PETTICOAT POLICY

PADMA K

INDIA • SINGAPORE • MALAYSIA

ISBN 979-8-89446-646-0

TO,

MOM

In the midst of all of her internal chaos, she loses sight of one critical fact. She is not only powerful, but she has an inner strength far beyond her realization.

She is the person everyone sees because every morning she wakes up and locks her darkest thoughts away. They don't beat her; she overcomes them.

Every single day the battle begins again, but she not only never fails to fight, she never fails to win. And that drive and willingness to sustain the fight makes her every bit as amazing on the inside as she appears on the outside. She maintains an impeccable veneer of calm and contentment.

Her smile is guaranteed to light up every room she enters. Not only does she remember every special occasion, but she's the first one to show up with a beautifully wrapped and thought-out gift.

She's not just the first one to volunteer, but she stays afterward to clean up and make sure everyone has a safe way home. On the surface, her life is perfect. She has it

all. Everything happens as if she planned her life down to the millisecond.

She is a role model not just for young women, but for all. By all accounts, she is flawless.

But what people fail to realize is that she oozes power and confidence because that is precisely the persona she wants the world to see. It's because she's strong and successful.

But little do they know, that's exactly what she decides to display of her. But behind her carefully constructed wall lies a heart that is holding in the darkness she doesn't want the world to see.

Her pain is locked away, deep down in places nobody could find. And even if they did scratch the surface of her pain, there is no way they could fathom the depths of her sorrow.

After all, why would anyone think she even can feel pain when all anyone sees is energetic bliss?

The only way anyone could begin to comprehend her pain would be to see her at that moment when she collapses on the bed all alone, the darkness her only companion.

She seeks solace in sleep, but the nightmares chase away any chance of relief. Her vulnerabilities bubble to the surface, and it is all she can do not to drown.

She chooses to suffer the slings and arrows of life in solitude, assuming a burden that nobody should have to endure alone. Her resistance comes not from a place of vanity or narcissism but from abject fear.

Because everyone believes she is living her best life without any effort or struggle, she does everything in her power to fulfill that perception. Ironically, her perfect life is the roadblock to that very goal.

To my mum with Love

Padmashree

CONTENTS

INTRODUCTION

As we traverse the intricate labyrinth of societal norms and traditions, the quest for gender equality remains an ongoing struggle. "Petticoat Policy" is a riveting exploration of this struggle, dissecting the complex layers of gender bias and discrimination that persist in our world. It is a timely discourse on the persistent issue of gender inequality, an age-old ailment that has gnawed at the fabric of societies worldwide.

This book is an unflinching examination of the roles, rights, and responsibilities traditionally associated with each gender, and how these age-old perceptions continue to influence our modern society. It delves into the heart of the inequality conundrum, highlighting the subtleties of gender bias that often go unnoticed, yet are deeply ingrained in our collective psyche.

"Petticoat Policy" is an eye-opening journey into the politics of gender, dissecting the struggles for equal rights and opportunities that have characterized human history. It aims to shine a spotlight on the challenges faced by women and men in their pursuit of equality, highlighting the systemic and institutionalized biases that continue to permeate our societies.

Through a unique blend of historical analysis, personal narratives, and future projections, "Petticoat Policy" seeks to unravel the intricacies of gender politics in our world today. It serves as a clarion call for societal introspection and change, urging readers to question, challenge, and ultimately dismantle the archaic norms that continue to perpetuate gender inequality.

The goal of this book is not to assign blame or point fingers, but to foster understanding and inspire action. It is a call to arms for all who believe in equal rights and opportunities, irrespective of gender. By shedding light on the often-overlooked aspects of gender inequality, "Petticoat Policy" hopes to stimulate meaningful conversations that will propel us towards a more equitable and inclusive future.

In the pages that follow, you will find food for thought, a catalyst for change, and perhaps, a blueprint for a world where gender equality is not just a lofty ideal, but a lived reality.

INVISIBLE CHAINS

The Social Labyrinth

In the vast maze of society, navigating the intricacies of social norms, expectations, and roles can be akin to traversing a labyrinth. This is especially true when it comes to the position of women, who are often subjected to a unique set of challenges and pressures. The term "petticoat policy" is a nod to the historical connotations of women's influence and power being exerted subtly, behind the scenes. It offers a compelling lens through which to explore the often-overlooked complexities of women's social experiences.

Consider the expectations placed upon women. There is an unspoken rulebook, a coded language of behavior that women are expected to adhere to. It is a dance of propriety, of maintaining the delicate balance between being assertive yet not aggressive, confident but not conceited, and ambitious without being perceived as threatening. Women are often expected to navigate this convoluted path, akin to the winding corridors of a labyrinth, with elegance and grace.

The social labyrinth that women navigate is not just about personal interactions; it extends to the professional sphere as well. Even in the 21st century, women are still grossly underrepresented in positions of power and influence. The glass ceiling phenomenon, the invisible barrier that prevents women from rising to the highest echelons of power in their careers, is a testament to this. It is a part of the social labyrinth that is particularly challenging to navigate, requiring not just skill and determination, but also an ability to challenge and subvert societal norms.

The labyrinth is not just external; it is internal as well. Women are often socialized to internalize certain beliefs and attitudes about themselves. They are taught to doubt their abilities, to downplay their achievements, to prioritize the needs of others over their own. This internal labyrinth can be just as, if not more, difficult to navigate than the external one. It requires a level of self-awareness and introspection that can be challenging to cultivate.

One might argue that the social labyrinth is not exclusive to women, that men too face their own set of social expectations and pressures. This is undoubtedly true. However, the labyrinth that women navigate is unique in its complexity and its implications. It is shaped by centuries of patriarchy, of societal norms and expectations that privilege men and disadvantage women. It is a labyrinth that is continually shifting, evolving with societal changes, yet its fundamental structure remains the same.

Navigating the social labyrinth is not just about survival; it is about resistance, about challenging and subverting the norms and expectations that confine women. It is about carving out a path, however winding and convoluted it may be, towards equality and empowerment. It is about recognizing the power and influence of the Petticoat policy and using it as a tool for change.

The social labyrinth is not just a challenge; it is an opportunity. It is an opportunity for women to assert their power and influence, to challenge and subvert the patriarchal norms that confine them. It is an opportunity to redefine what it means to be a woman in the 21st century, to rewrite the rulebook, to reshape the labyrinth itself. It is an opportunity to redefine the petticoat policy, to transform it from a symbol of subtle, behind-the-scenes influence to a symbol of overt, unapologetic power.

Silent Voices

Consider for a moment, the countless women whose voices have been silenced, their contributions overlooked, and their potential stifled due to the iron grip of the petticoat policy. This policy, deeply ingrained in our society, has resulted in an unconscious bias against women, suppressing their voices and hindering their progress. The second chapter of our discourse, Silent Voices, aims to shed light on this tragic reality and persuade you to join the fight against this unfair policy.

The Petticoat policy, a phrase often used to denote the gender bias in our society, is not a new phenomenon. It has been lurking in the shadows, shaping our society and its norms for centuries. It has silenced the voices of women, belittled their achievements, and confined them to roles deemed suitable by a patriarchal society. This policy has not only curtailed the potential of women but has also hampered the progress of our society as a whole.

Imagine a world where every voice matters, where every individual, regardless of their gender, has an equal opportunity to contribute to society. Sounds utopian, doesn't it? However, this is not an impossible dream. We can shatter the glass ceiling of the petticoat policy and create a society where everyone's voice is heard, and where every contribution is valued.

By raising awareness about the Petticoat policy, we can encourage more people to challenge it. We need to question the norms that have been handed down to us, to scrutinize them, and to discard them if they prove to be unjust. We need to listen to the silent voices, the voices that the Petticoat policy has tried to muffle. We need to acknowledge their struggles, their achievements, and their potential. Only then can we hope to dismantle the Petticoat policy.

Furthermore, we need to educate our younger generations about the Petticoat policy. They need to understand its implications and its effects. They need to be prepared to challenge it, to fight against it. We need to instill in them a sense of justice and equality, so they can build a society that is free from the shackles of the Petticoat policy.

Moreover, we need to empower women. We need to give them the tools they need to fight against the Petticoat policy. We need to encourage them to raise their voices, to make their voices heard. We need to support them in their fight for equality. We need to stand with them, to fight with them.

The Petticoat policy is not just a women's issue. It is a societal issue. It affects us all, directly or indirectly. By silencing the voices of women, we are silencing half of our society. We are stunting our growth, and our progress. We are denying ourselves the chance to reach our full potential.

Therefore, let us challenge the Petticoat policy. Let us listen to the silent voices. Let us stand together, united in our fight for equality. Let us create a society where every voice matters, and where every contribution is valued. Let us break the chains of the Petticoat policy and let the silent voices be heard.

Behind the Glass Ceiling

The world of business and politics has long been a male-dominated sphere. Women, although making impressive strides in recent years, still face a significant barrier in their quest for equality. This barrier, often referred to as the 'glass ceiling,' is an invisible yet powerful force that prevents women from reaching the top echelons of their respective fields.

Consider the world of business. Despite women making up roughly half of the global workforce, they only comprise a small fraction of CEOs and top executives. The same goes for politics, where women are grossly underrepresented in positions of power. The question arises, why is this the case? The answer lies in the persistent, systemic biases ingrained in our societies and institutions.

Women are often seen as less competent than men, regardless of their qualifications or achievements. This is not due to any inherent lack of ability, but rather societal stereotypes that perceive women as being less capable. This perception is perpetuated by the media, which often portrays women in stereotypically feminine roles, reinforcing the notion that women are not fit for leadership positions.

Moreover, women are often expected to conform to traditional gender roles, which include being nurturing, caring, and submissive. These expectations can make it difficult for women to assert themselves and be recognized as leaders. They may also be penalized for exhibiting traits that are typically associated with successful leadership, such as assertiveness and decisiveness.

Another significant obstacle women face is the lack of mentorship and sponsorship opportunities. Mentorship is crucial for career advancement, as it provides guidance, support, and opportunities for growth. However, women often lack access to these opportunities, as most mentors and sponsors are men who are more likely to mentor other men.

Furthermore, women are often held to higher standards than their male counterparts. They are expected to perform exceptionally well to prove their worth, while men are often given the benefit of the doubt. This double standard places an undue burden on women, making it even more difficult for them to break through the glass ceiling.

However, this does not mean that the situation is hopeless. On the contrary, there are countless examples of women who have shattered the glass ceiling and achieved remarkable success in their respective fields. These women serve as role models and inspirations for countless others, proving that it is indeed possible to overcome these barriers.

The key to breaking through the glass ceiling lies in challenging and dismantling the systemic biases that uphold it. This requires a collective effort from all members of society, not just women. It involves challenging societal stereotypes, promoting gender equality, and creating opportunities for women to thrive in leadership roles.

Furthermore, organizations can play a significant role in facilitating this change. They can implement policies that promote gender equality, provide mentorship and sponsorship opportunities for women, and create a culture that values diversity and inclusion.

The glass ceiling may be a daunting obstacle, but it is not insurmountable. With determination, perseverance, and the right support, women can and will break through it. After all, the view from the top is worth the climb.

Unseen Labor

In the vast tapestry of human history, women have been the threads holding it together, often underappreciated and overlooked. Their work, their contributions, their struggles, often remain unseen and unacknowledged. This is no less true in the realm of policy-making, where women's efforts often constitute the invisible labor that keeps the wheels of progress turning.

Imagine the countless hours women have spent drafting, revising, and implementing policies. Think of the numerous sleepless nights spent researching, the countless meetings attended, the endless paperwork filled, all to ensure that policies are effective, equitable, and just. Yet, this immense labor often goes unnoticed, and unrecognized. It's time to shed light on this unseen labor.

The policy-making process is a complex one, filled with intricate negotiations, tactical maneuvering, and careful planning. It requires the ability to listen, to compromise, to stand firm when necessary, and to adapt when circumstances demand. Women, with their innate ability to multitask, to empathize, to build consensus, are well-suited for this demanding task. Yet, their work often remains in the shadows, not because it is insignificant, but because it is often taken for granted.

The long hours spent poring over policy documents, the painstaking attention to detail required in drafting legislation, the emotional labor involved in mediating disputes and finding common ground – these are not tasks that can be quantified or easily seen. But they are tasks that are vital to the functioning of our society. Without this unseen labor, our policy-making process would grind to a halt.

Moreover, women's unseen labor in policy-making extends beyond the actual drafting and implementing of policies. It encompasses the emotional and mental effort required to navigate a predominantly male-dominated field, to push for change in the face of resistance, to advocate for policies that promote gender equality and social justice. This labor, too, is often unseen and unrecognized.

Yet, this unseen labor is not without its rewards. The satisfaction of seeing a policy you've worked on come to fruition, the pride in knowing that your efforts have contributed to positive change, the gratification of seeing the impact of your work on the lives of others – these are rewards that cannot be quantified or measured. But they are rewards that are deeply meaningful and fulfilling.

The time has come to acknowledge and value the unseen labor of women in policy-making. Their contributions are invaluable, their efforts indispensable. Without them, our society would not be the place it is today. Let us not take their work for granted any longer. Let us recognize and appreciate the unseen labor of women in policy-making, for it is this labor that shapes our world, that drives progress, that makes a difference.

To dismiss this labor as insignificant or unimportant is to dismiss the crucial role women play in our society. It is to undermine the progress we have made in promoting gender equality and social justice. It is to ignore the countless ways in which women contribute to our society and our world. Let us not fall into this trap. Let us recognize and appreciate the unseen labor of women in policy-making. It's time to bring this unseen labor into the light.

HISTORY'S FORGOTTEN

Invisible Builders

In the grand tapestry of civilization, there are countless threads that intertwine, each one playing its part in creating the intricate design we call society. Yet, there are certain threads that, despite their influential role, remain hidden, unacknowledged, and unappreciated. These are the invisible builders, the women who have shaped, and continue to shape, the world we live in from behind the scenes.

Consider this: The world's first computer programmer was a woman, Ada Lovelace. The structure of DNA was discovered by a woman, Rosalind Franklin. The first novel ever written was by a woman, Murasaki Shikibu. Yet, how often are these names mentioned in the annals of history? How often do we celebrate their contributions, their innovations, their genius?

Women, for centuries, have been the invisible builders of our society. They have worked tirelessly, innovating and creating, only for their achievements to be dismissed, downplayed, or outright stolen. They have been the architects of progress, the engineers of change, yet their work often goes unacknowledged and their voices unheard.

Consider the countless mothers whose nurturing has raised generations of leaders, thinkers, and doers. The teachers who have educated and inspired, the nurses who have cared and healed, the scientists who have discovered and innovated. These are the invisible builders, the women whose contributions from the bedrock of our society.

Yet, despite their pivotal role, women are often sidelined, their work underappreciated and their voices silenced. They are expected to work twice as hard for half the recognition, to fight for a seat at the table, to prove their worth in a world that often takes them for granted.

This is the Petticoat policy, the systemic marginalization of women and their contributions. It is a policy that has been in place for centuries, a policy that continues to pervade our society, a policy that we must challenge and dismantle.

Let us consider the invisible builders, the women who have shaped our world from behind the scenes. Let us acknowledge their contributions, celebrate their achievements, and give them the recognition they deserve. Let us reject the petty coat policy, the systemic marginalization of women and their contributions. Let us strive for a world where all builders are acknowledged, where all voices are heard, where all contributions are valued.

The invisible builders, the women who have shaped our world, deserve more than our acknowledgment. They deserve our respect, our admiration, our gratitude.

They deserve to have their work celebrated, their achievements recognized, their names remembered.

We must challenge the petty coat policy, the systemic marginalization of women and their contributions. We must acknowledge the invisible builders, the women who have shaped our world from behind the scenes. We must celebrate their achievements, their innovations, their genius.

The invisible builders, the women who have shaped our world, are not just a part of our history. They are a part of our present, and they will be a part of our future. Let us ensure that their contributions are acknowledged, their voices are heard, and their work is celebrated. Let us ensure that the petty coat policy is relegated to the annals of history, a reminder of a time when we failed to value all of our builders. Let us strive for a world where all builders are acknowledged, where all voices are heard, where all contributions are valued.

Silent Revolutionaries

Often, the most profound changes are not those that are announced with grand fanfare, but those that quietly, subtly, redefine the fabric of our society. In the realm of politics, it is sometimes the silent revolutionaries who bring about the most enduring transformations. This notion is especially true when we turn our gaze towards the women who have shaped, and continue to shape, the political landscape. They are the unsung heroes, the quiet powerhouses, the 'petticoat policymakers' who have brought about a seismic shift in the realm of governance.

This is not a tale of the women who have made headlines, who have graced magazine covers or whose speeches have reverberated through the halls of power. Instead, it is a testament to those who have worked behind the scenes, whose influence, though often overlooked, has been no less significant.

Consider the women who, throughout history, have been the wives, the mothers, the sisters, and the daughters of politicians. These women have wielded their influence not from the podium, but from the domestic sphere. They have shaped policy not through public speeches, but through private conversations. They have been the confidantes, the advisors, the sounding boards for the men who have held the reins of power. Their influence, though unacknowledged, has been profound.

Yet, it is not just these women who deserve our attention. The women who serve as the administrative backbone of political parties, the campaign strategists, the policy researchers, the speechwriters, they too are part of this silent revolution. They may not be the faces of the campaign, but without their tireless work, their strategic insight, their wordsmithing prowess, the political machinery would grind to a halt.

And let us not forget the women who have dared to enter the political arena themselves. Not the women who have risen to the top, but those who have contested elections at the grassroots level, who have served on town councils, school boards, and local committees. These women, through their everyday work, their dedication to their communities, their unwavering commitment to public service, have challenged the status quo. They have shown that politics is not a man's domain, that women too have a place in the decision-making process.

The path these women have tread is not an easy one. They have faced, and continue to face, numerous hurdles. Sexism, misogyny, discrimination, these are just some of the obstacles they have had to overcome. Yet, they have persevered. They have refused to be silenced. They have continued to fight, to push for change, to make their voices heard.

These women, these silent revolutionaries, are the embodiment of the petticoat policy. They have shown that power is not just found in the halls of government, but also in the home, in the office, in the community. They have shown that influence is not just about public recognition, but about quiet persistence, about the courage to keep pushing, even when the odds are stacked against you.

The silent revolutionaries of the petticoat policy are a testament to the power of women in politics. They may not always be in the spotlight, but their influence is undeniable. They are the unsung heroes, the quiet powerhouses, the women who are reshaping the political landscape, one policy, one conversation, one election at a time.

Erased Contributions

Often, the most significant parts of history are those that are left untold. This is particularly true when it comes to the contributions of women in shaping the world we live in today. This part of history is often overlooked, underappreciated, and unfortunately, erased.

Imagine a tapestry, intricately woven with threads of various colors, each representing a different contribution to society. Now picture many of these threads being ignored, their colors fading into the background, their significance lost. This is the reality of the contributions of women throughout history. They have been the unsung heroes, working behind the scenes, their contributions significant but often unrecognized and unrecorded.

Consider the realms of science, literature, and politics. Women such as Marie Curie, Jane Austen, and Eleanor Roosevelt have made monumental contributions in their respective fields. Yet, they are often overshadowed by their male counterparts. Marie Curie, despite her groundbreaking research in radioactivity, is often a footnote in the annals of scientific history. Jane Austen, despite her literary genius, is often dismissed as a writer of 'women's novels'. Eleanor Roosevelt, despite her role as a driving force in the creation of the Universal Declaration of Human Rights, is often remembered merely as a First Lady.

The erasure of women's contributions is not just unjust; it also deprives us of role models and inspirations. When we fail to acknowledge the achievements of women, we send a message to the younger generation that women are incapable of making meaningful contributions. This is not just unfair; it is also untrue. Women have always been capable of greatness, and it is high time we start recognizing this.

Moreover, the erasure of women's contributions distorts our understanding of history and society. It paints a picture that is incomplete and skewed. To truly understand our past and build a better future, we must recognize and value the contributions of all members of society, regardless of their gender.

The erasure of women's contributions is a symptom of a larger problem: gender inequality. It is a reflection of the patriarchal norms that have dominated our society for centuries. These norms have dictated that women's roles are limited to the private sphere, while men dominate the public sphere. This is a narrative that we must challenge and change.

However, change is not easy. It requires us to confront deeply entrenched beliefs and prejudices. It requires us to question the status quo and demand for a more equitable and inclusive society. But it is a change that is necessary and long overdue.

As we move forward, let us remember the women who have paved the way for us. Let us honor their contributions by ensuring that they are not erased from history. Let us strive for a society where the contributions of all, regardless of their gender, are recognized and valued.

The erasure of women's contributions is not just a historical issue; it is a contemporary issue that we must address. By doing so, we take a step towards creating a more equitable and just society, a society where the contributions of all are recognized and valued. This is the society that we must strive for, and this is the society that we can and must achieve.

The petty coat policy has no place in our world. Let's unravel it, thread by thread, until the tapestry of history is complete and true.

Hidden Heroines

As we delve deeper into the intricate fabric of history, it becomes increasingly apparent that the role of women, enshrouded in mystery and often overlooked, is far more significant than traditionally believed. In the shadows of great men and their celebrated feats, a multitude of women have been silently shaping the world, their contributions often neglected and their names forgotten. This chapter seeks to rectify this oversight, shedding light on these hidden heroines and the indelible imprints they have left on the annals of history.

The women we will explore in this chapter are not simply the wives, daughters or mothers of influential men; they are, in their own right, pioneers, visionaries, and trailblazers. These women, often forced to navigate the treacherous waters of a male-dominated world, have managed to make lasting contributions to society, politics, and culture. Their legacies, albeit often hidden, are woven into the fabric of our global heritage.

Consider the case of Rosalind Franklin, a chemist whose work was instrumental in the discovery of the structure of DNA. While Watson and Crick are often celebrated for this scientific breakthrough, it was Franklin's meticulous research and strikingly accurate x-ray images that laid the foundation for their success. Yet, her name was largely forgotten, her contributions overshadowed by her male counterparts.

Similarly, countless women have made significant contributions to the political sphere, often working behind the scenes to enact change. Consider the Suffragettes, who fought tirelessly for women's right to vote. Many of these women, like Emmeline Pankhurst, are remembered for their leadership. However, thousands of other women, whose names have been lost to history, also played crucial roles in this movement. They risked their lives and their reputations, facing prison and public condemnation, to ensure a more equitable future for all women.

In the realm of art and culture, women have long been relegated to the role of muse, their own creative endeavors often overlooked or dismissed. Yet, women like Mary Cassatt, Artemisia Gentileschi, and Zora Neale Hurston have defied societal expectations, creating works of art and literature that continue to influence and inspire today. Their work, often created in the face of adversity and prejudice, serves as a testament to the resilience and creativity of women.

These stories serve as a poignant reminder of the countless women who have been left out of our history books, their contributions minimized or forgotten. However, it is not enough to simply acknowledge their existence. We must actively work to bring their stories to light, to honor their contributions, and to ensure that future generations understand the full breadth and depth of women's influence on our world.

The women of the past, the hidden heroines who have shaped our world, deserve to be remembered. Their courage, intelligence, and resilience serve as a powerful reminder of women's potential and the importance of their inclusion in all aspects of life. As we continue to uncover their stories, we begin to see a complete and more balanced picture of our shared history, one that truly reflects the contributions of all its participants.

In the grand tapestry of history, every thread matters. Let us not forget the threads spun by these hidden heroines, for they are integral to the richness and diversity of our shared past. Their stories, full of strength and resilience, are a testament to the power of women and a call to action for us all: to recognize, honor, and celebrate the often-overlooked contributions of women throughout history.

THE FIGHT FOR EQUALITY

Breaking Barriers

The world we live in has always been a stage for struggle and conflict, a constant battle to break free from the chains of limitations and prejudices. This is especially true for women, who have been subjected to societal constraints and expectations for centuries. The 'petticoat policy' is a metaphorical representation of the restrictions imposed on women, especially in the professional world. This policy, however, is not a written law or a decreed ordinance; it is a silent, unwritten rule that has been passed down from generation to generation.

The 'petticoat policy' is not a new phenomenon. It has been present in societies worldwide for centuries, subtly influencing the roles and expectations of women. It is a reflection of a patriarchal society that has long held the reins of power and control. However, the time has come to challenge this policy, to break the barriers it has imposed, and to usher in an era of equality and justice.

Breaking barriers is not an easy task. It requires courage, resilience, and an unwavering belief in oneself. It is about standing tall in the face of adversity and refusing to bow down to societal pressures. It is about challenging the status quo and daring to dream of a world where women are not confined to the shadows of their male counterparts.

Women are not just nurturers or caregivers; they are leaders, innovators, and trailblazers. They have the potential to excel in any field, be it politics, science, technology, or arts. Yet, they are often overlooked, their talents unrecognized, their voices unheard. This is what the 'petticoat policy' does; it silences women, it marginalizes them, it attempts to confine them within a box.

Breaking these barriers is not just about achieving personal success; it is about paving the way for future generations. It is about creating a world where a woman's worth is not judged by her gender, but by her abilities, her skills, and her contributions to society. It is about ensuring that every girl, regardless of her background, has the opportunity to reach her full potential.

Challenging the 'petticoat policy' is a collective responsibility. It is not a battle to be fought alone; it is a movement that requires the support and participation of everyone. Men need to be allies in this fight, standing shoulder to shoulder with women in their quest for equality. They need to recognize the role they play in perpetuating these barriers and take active steps to dismantle them.

Furthermore, society needs to shed its preconceived notions about gender roles. It needs to acknowledge the strength and capability of women, and celebrate their achievements. It needs to reject the stereotypes that have been ingrained in our minds and embrace the reality of a world where women are equal partners.

Breaking barriers is not just a dream; it is a necessity. It is a call to action, a rallying cry for change. It is a journey towards a more equitable and just society, where the 'petticoat policy' is a thing of the past. It is a fight for freedom, for dignity, and for respect. It is a fight that we cannot afford to lose.

Shattering Stereotypes

In the realm of women's political participation, we often find ourselves ensnared by preconceived notions and stereotypes. The notion that politics is a man's world, and that women are best suited for roles that are nurturing and supportive, is an antiquated stereotype that needs to be shattered. We must move past these misconceptions and forge a path towards a more inclusive and equitable political arena.

Let's first examine the stereotype that asserts that women are too emotional to handle politics. This belief is flawed and unfounded. Emotion is not a sign of weakness, but of strength. It is a testament to an individual's capacity for empathy, compassion, and understanding - traits that are essential for ethical and effective leadership. Women do not lack the ability to make rational decisions; they just have the added advantage of being able to factor in emotional intelligence, which can lead to more comprehensive and considerate decisions.

Next, we need to challenge the stereotype that women are not assertive or competitive enough for politics. Women are just as capable of being assertive and competitive as men, if not more so. Our society has conditioned women to be accommodating and agreeable, but this does not mean they lack the ability to be assertive when required. In fact, women are often more adept at managing conflicts and finding solutions, as they are more likely to take into account the needs and perspectives of all parties involved.

Another stereotype that needs to be shattered is the idea that women lack the knowledge or interest to participate in politics. This is simply not true. Women have consistently proven their intellectual prowess and capacity for critical thinking. They are just as capable of understanding and engaging with complex political issues as men. Moreover, women bring unique perspectives and insights to the table, due to their different lived experiences.

The perception that politics is a dirty game and women should remain untainted by it also needs to be dismantled. Politics is not inherently dirty or corrupt. It is the actions of individuals that determine the nature of politics. Women, with their strong ethical compass and commitment to fairness, can bring about a much-needed change in the political landscape.

Lastly, the stereotype that women do not have the time for politics due to their domestic responsibilities needs to be debunked. The concept of women as the primary caregivers and homemakers is a socially constructed one. Women have the same right to personal and professional fulfillment as men. It is about time we create a society where both men and women share domestic responsibilities equally, freeing up time for women to participate in politics.

It is high time we shatter these stereotypes and pave the way for more women to step into the political arena. Women have the potential to bring about significant positive changes in the world of politics. Their leadership can lead to more empathetic, ethical, and effective governance. Let's strive towards creating a political landscape that celebrates diversity and inclusion, one that gives women the space and respect they deserve.

The Struggle for Rights

In the realm of social and political evolution, the struggle for rights has been a pivotal force. It has been the catalyst for change, the spark that ignites the flames of revolution. Women have been at the forefront of this struggle, a testament to their resolve and resilience as they grappled with the chains of societal norms.

The narrative of the petticoat Policy is not a tale of the weak or the submissive. It is a saga of strength, of courage, and of unyielding determination. Women, draped in their petticoats, have been the silent warriors, the unsung heroes in the fight for equality and justice. They have been the architects of their destiny, shaping the course of history with their indomitable spirit.

The Petticoat Policy is a poignant reminder of the struggle women have endured for their rights. Their fight is not just about gaining the right to vote or the right to work. It is about the recognition of their humanity, their dignity, and their worth. It is about demanding respect, equality, and justice in a world that has often treated them as second-class citizens.

As we leaf through the pages of history, we find countless examples of women who have defied societal norms and expectations to fight for their rights. They have braved ridicule, scorn, and persecution to make their voices heard. These women did not just fight for themselves, but for the future generations of women who would come after them.

In the face of adversity, these women did not falter. They did not bow down to the oppressive forces that sought to silence them. Instead, they rose, like phoenixes from the ashes, stronger and more determined than ever. They fought with every ounce of their being, with every fiber of their soul, to make a difference.

The Petticoat Policy is not just a story of women's struggle for rights. It is a testament to their resilience, their courage, and their unwavering determination. It is a tribute to the countless women who have fought and continue to fight, for their rights.

The Petticoat Policy is a call to action. It is a call for us to acknowledge the struggles and sacrifices of these women, to honor their bravery and their resilience. It is a call for us to stand up for what is right, fight for equality and justice, challenge the status quo, and demand change.

The struggle for rights is not over. It is a battle that continues to be fought, a battle that requires our collective effort and resolve. The Petticoat Policy is a beacon of hope, a beacon that guides us in this ongoing struggle. It is a reminder of the power of determination, of the strength that lies within each one of us, and of the change that we can bring about when we stand together.

Let us not forget the lessons of the petticoat Policy. Let us honor the women who have paved the way for us, and let us continue their fight for rights. Let us be the change we want to see in the world.

The Long March

From the heart of our narrative, we invite you to pause. Pause and reflect on the path that has been trodden, the miles that have been covered, the hurdles that have been jumped. This is not a mere recounting of events; this is a testament to resilience, a tribute to the tenacity of those who dared to defy the status quo, to challenge the 'petticoat policy' that sought to confine them within societal constructs.

The long march, as we call it, is not a physical journey. It is not about the number of steps taken, but rather the strength of the strides. It is about the spirit of defiance that fueled each step, the courage that propelled each move, the determination that drove each decision.

Each footfall echoed with the demand for equality, for the right to wear trousers in a world that insisted petticoats. Each step was a silent protest, a declaration of autonomy, a repudiation of the norms that sought to dictate their lives. They moved not as a crowd, but as a force, a force driven by the collective will to challenge, to change, to conquer.

Challenging the 'petticoat policy' was not a simple task. It meant standing up against centuries of traditions, deeply ingrained beliefs, against societal expectations. It meant facing ridicule, enduring criticism, and braving ostracism. But they did not falter. They did not retreat. They held their heads high, squared their shoulders, and marched on.

Their march was not confined to the physical realm. It extended to the intellectual landscape, where they challenged the stereotypes that sought to define them, the prejudices that sought to belittle them, the biases that sought to marginalize them. They questioned, they debated, they argued. They made their voices heard, their presence felt, their power acknowledged.

The long march was not a solitary battle. It was a collective effort, a shared struggle, a joint endeavor. They stood together, supported each other, buoyed each other. They celebrated their victories, mourned their losses, and drew strength from their shared experiences. They were not just a group of individuals; they were a community, a sisterhood, a force to be reckoned with.

Their march continues. The 'petticoat policy' may have evolved, but the fight for equality persists. The hurdles may have changed, but the resilience remains. The battles may have shifted, but the spirit of defiance endures. The long march is not a chapter in history; it is a living testament to the power of perseverance, the strength of solidarity, and the resilience of resistance.

We invite you to pause, not to rest, but to reflect. Reflect on the strides that have been made, the battles that have been won, the progress that has been achieved. But do not stop. The march is not over. The fight is not won. The journey continues.

The 'petticoat policy' may be a relic of the past, but its legacy lingers. The long march is not just a part of history; it is a call to action, a challenge to complacency, a reminder of the power of resistance. So, stand tall, step forward, and march on.

THE POWER OF WOMEN

CHAPTER

04

Strength in Adversity

It is through the crucible of adversity that true strength is forged. The fiery trials we face, the obstacles we overcome, the battles we bravely fight, all serve to mold us into stronger, more resilient beings. This is a fundamental truth that resonates throughout "Petty coat Policy", echoing in the lives of the remarkable women whose stories are woven into its pages.

These women did not shy away from adversity. Instead, they faced it head-on, with a courage and resolve that can only be admired. They were not born into positions of power or privilege, but through their strength and determination, they carved out a place for themselves in a world that often sought to limit their potential.

Consider, for instance, the story of Margaret, a seamstress who found herself in the throes of poverty after the death of her husband. Instead of succumbing to despair, she harnessed her skills and started her own business, despite the societal norms that frowned upon women in entrepreneurship. She faced adversity and, through her strength, emerged victorious.

Or take the case of Elizabeth, a young woman who dared to dream of a career in politics, at a time when women were largely excluded from the political arena. She faced rejections, ridicule, and scorn, but she did not let these deter her. Instead, she used them as stepping stones on her path to success, proving that strength can indeed be born out of adversity.

These women, and many others like them, serve as powerful reminders that adversity should not be viewed as an insurmountable obstacle, but rather as an opportunity for growth and empowerment. Their strength in the face of adversity is a testament to their resilience, a trait that is all too often undervalued in our society.

We live in a world that tends to glorify success and shun failure, that rewards victory and overlooks the battles fought. But it is through adversity that we truly learn what we are made of, that we discover our inner strength and resilience. It is through adversity that we are given the chance to prove ourselves, to rise above our circumstances and achieve greatness.

The women in "Petty coat Policy" did not let adversity define them. Instead, they used it as a catalyst for change, a tool for empowerment. They turned their trials into triumphs, their obstacles into opportunities. They proved that strength can indeed be found in adversity, and that it is this strength that allows us to overcome, to persevere, and to succeed.

So, as you delve into the pages of "Petty coat Policy", let these women's stories inspire you. Let them remind you that adversity is not something to be feared, but rather something to be faced with courage and resolve. Let them show you that you too, can find strength in adversity, that you too, can turn your trials into triumphs.

Remember, it is not the absence of adversity that defines us, but rather how we respond to it. So, face your challenges with courage, with determination, and with the knowledge that you are stronger than you think. Because, as the women in "Petty coat Policy" have shown us, there is indeed strength in adversity.

Resilience and Resolve

In the world of politics, the ability to bounce back from adversity and maintain a determined spirit is vital. The political landscape can be a daunting place, especially for those who are not accustomed to the cutthroat nature of this environment. It is in this realm that resilience and resolve become essential tools for survival.

Imagine a woman stepping into this arena, clad not in armor, but in a petticoat. She navigates through policies and power plays, her feminine attire not a sign of weakness, but rather an emblem of her strength and determination. This is not a tale of fiction; it is the reality for many women who have chosen to take on the challenge of political leadership.

Resilience is not about avoiding hardship; it's about facing it head-on and coming out stronger on the other side. It's about learning from one's mistakes and using them as stepping stones towards success. For a woman in politics, this could mean enduring sexist comments, overcoming gender bias, or fighting against discriminatory practices. Yet, despite these obstacles, she remains steadfast, knowing that her journey is not just about her, but about paving the way for future generations of women leaders.

Resolve, on the other hand, is the unwavering determination to achieve one's goals, no matter the hurdles that stand in the way. It's about having a clear vision and sticking to it, even when others try to sway you away from your path. In politics, this could mean standing up for policies that may not be popular but are necessary for the greater good. It's about making tough decisions and standing by them, knowing that you're acting in the best interest of those you represent.

The Petticoat, often viewed as a symbol of femininity and fragility, takes on a new meaning in the context of politics. It becomes a symbol of resilience and resolve, representing the strength and determination of women who dare to step into the political arena.

Women in politics face a unique set of challenges, but it is their resilience and resolve that enable them to overcome these obstacles and make a significant impact. They stand firm in the face of adversity, refusing to be swayed by the winds of change. They remain committed to their cause, not allowing anyone or anything to deter them from their path.

These qualities are not exclusive to women; they are traits that anyone can cultivate, regardless of gender.

However, in the context of the petticoat policy, they hold special significance. They serve as a reminder that one's attire does not determine one's strength or ability. It is one's character, resilience, and resolve that truly matter.

Women in politics are not merely surviving; they are thriving, breaking barriers, and making strides in areas once dominated by men. They are rewriting the narrative, proving that the petticoat is not a symbol of weakness, but a testament to their resilience and resolve.

The Petticoat policy is not just about women in politics; it's a call to action for everyone. It's a plea for resilience in the face of adversity, for resolve in the pursuit of one's goals. It's a message of empowerment, reminding us all that we are capable of far more than we think. It's a testament to the power of the petticoat, and the strength of the women who wear them.

The Power of Persistence

Consider the power of persistence, a force so potent that it can transform mere dreams into reality. It is this unwavering tenacity that can propel us forward, overcoming adversity and achieving the seemingly impossible. In the realm of the petticoat Policy, this steadfast will is not just an asset, it is a necessity.

The Petticoat Policy, a term that encapsulates the struggles and triumphs of women in politics, is not merely about gender equality. It is about the resilience, the determination, and the unyielding spirit of women who refuse to back down, no matter how daunting the circumstances. It is a testament to the power of persistence, and a lesson for all who dare to dream big.

Persistence does not mean merely staying in the fight, it means thriving in it. It is the grit that keeps you going when the odds are stacked against you, the resilience that helps you bounce back from failure, and the tenacity that fuels you to keep pushing forward, no matter how steep the climb. Without persistence, the world would be devoid of change-makers and trailblazers, people who dared to challenge the status quo and make a difference.

The Petticoat Policy is a testament to the power of persistence. It tells the tales of women who dared to enter the daunting world of politics, a domain traditionally dominated by men. These women did not merely survive in this domain, they thrived. They faced adversity head-on, refused to back down in the face of challenges, and remained steadfast in their commitment to their cause. They are the embodiment of persistence, and their stories are a testament to the power of this trait.

Consider for a moment, the woman who runs for office despite being told she doesn't have a chance, the woman who fights for a cause she believes in, even when the world tells her it's a lost cause, or the woman who refuses to back down, even when the odds are stacked against her. These are the women of the petticoat Policy, the women who have harnessed the power of persistence to make a difference in the world.

The power of persistence cannot be underestimated. It is a force that can propel us forward, help us overcome adversity, and transform our dreams into reality. It is a trait that is not just valuable, but essential, in the realm of thePettycoat Policy.

So let us celebrate the power of persistence. Let us applaud the women who have harnessed this power to make a difference in the world. Let us learn from their stories, be inspired by their courage, and strive to emulate their tenacity. For in the realm of the petticoat Policy, persistence is not just a trait, it is a way of life. It is the force that propels us forward, the grit that keeps us going, and the tenacity that fuels us to keep pushing, no matter how steep the climb. In the end, it is the power of persistence that can transform the seemingly impossible into the possible.

The Force of Femininity

When we ponder the true strength of femininity, it is essential to dispel the common misconceptions that often cloud our understanding. Femininity, in its purest form, is not weakness, vulnerability, or subservience. Instead, it is a powerful force that has the potential to shape society, influence policy, and inspire change.

Throughout history, women have been relegated to secondary roles, often overlooked and underestimated. Yet, it is this very underestimation that has allowed women to wield their influence subtly and effectively. Their power lies not in brute force or aggression, but in their ability to inspire, nurture, and create.

Consider the role of women in the family unit, for instance. They are often the primary caregivers, responsible for raising the next generation. Their values, beliefs, and attitudes shape the minds of young children, influencing their behavior and shaping their future. This is not a role to be taken lightly. The power to mold the future leaders of our world is a testament to the immense force of femininity.

Moreover, women have also demonstrated their strength in the professional realm. Despite facing significant barriers, they have broken through glass ceilings, proving their worth in fields traditionally dominated by men. They have shown that femininity does not equate to incompetence or inefficiency. Women can lead, innovate, and excel, all while maintaining their feminine traits.

Femininity is also a potent force in the realm of policy-making. The term 'petticoat policy' was often used derogatorily to refer to the influence of women on political decisions. However, this influence should not be dismissed or belittled. Women bring a unique perspective to the table, one that is often rooted in empathy, compassion, and a deep understanding of social issues. Their input is invaluable in creating policies that are inclusive, equitable, and sustainable.

The power of femininity is also evident in social movements. Women have been at the forefront of many significant changes, fighting for rights, equality, and justice. Their resilience, determination, and courage are a testament to the strength that lies in femininity. They have shown that they are not just victims of circumstance but active agents of change.

The force of femininity is not a threat to masculinity. It is not a challenge to the established order or a call for dominance. It is a call for recognition, for respect, for equality. It is a call to acknowledge the strength that lies in compassion, empathy, and nurturing. It is a call to embrace a different kind of power, one that is not rooted in aggression or dominance, but in understanding and collaboration.

Femininity is an inherent part of human nature, a force that has shaped our world in countless ways. It is a force that deserves to be celebrated, recognized, and valued. The strength of femininity is not in its ability to mimic masculinity but in its capacity to offer a different perspective, a different approach, and a different kind of power.

So, let us not underestimate the force of femininity. Let us not confine it to archaic stereotypes or dismiss it as a weakness. Let us recognize it for what it truly is - a potent force capable of inspiring change, influencing policy, and shaping the future.

THE FUTURE IS FEMALE

Shaping Tomorrow

Imagine a world where the policy is no longer dictated by the traditional power structures, a world where the petticoat is not merely a symbol of femininity but a symbol of power, change, and progress. This world can be our reality. We are at the cusp of a new era, an era of the petticoat policy.

The Petticoat policy is not just about women in power. It's about redefining power structures and the way we govern. It's about moving away from the aggressive, competitive, and hierarchical systems that have led to war, injustice, and environmental destruction. Instead, we embrace a new paradigm, one that values collaboration, empathy, and sustainability. A paradigm that sees power not as something to be hoarded but as something to be shared.

The Petticoat policy is about bringing the feminine perspective to the forefront. For centuries, our policies have been shaped by masculine values, leaving us with a world that is out of balance. Now, it's time to bring balance back by incorporating the feminine values of compassion, nurturing, and cooperation into our policies.

The Petticoat policy is not just for women. It's for everyone who believes in a more equitable, sustainable, and peaceful world. It's for those who understand that the future of our planet depends on our ability to work together, to respect each other, and to take care of our common home.

We are not advocating for a world where women dominate men. We are advocating for a world where everyone, regardless of their gender, has a voice. A world where decisions are made not by a select few but by everyone affected by them. A world where power is not a weapon but a tool for positive change.

The Petticoat policy is not a dream. It's a necessity. We are facing unprecedented challenges that require unprecedented solutions. We can no longer afford to rely on the same old ways of doing things. We need new ideas, new perspectives, and new leadership.

The Petticoat policy is the answer. It's a policy that values people over profits, relationships over transactions, and the planet over short-term gains. It's a policy that understands that we are all interconnected and that our actions have consequences. It's a policy that seeks to create a world that works for everyone, not just a privileged few.

The Petticoat policy is not a threat. It's an opportunity. An opportunity to create a more just, sustainable, and peaceful world. An opportunity to redefine power, to reshape policy, and to shape our future.

The Petticoat policy is our future. It's a future where everyone has a voice, where power is shared, and where our policies reflect our values. It's a future where the petticoat is not just a symbol of femininity but a symbol of power, change, and progress.

Join us in shaping this future. Join us in implementing the Petticoat policy. The future is not something that happens to us. It's something we create. So, let's create a future that works for everyone. Let's create a future shaped by the petticoat policy.

Leading the Charge

Undeniably, we are in the thick of an era where women are making strides in every domain, yet when it comes to leadership, there is still a significant gap. It is essential, now more than ever, for women to take the reins and pave the way for a more balanced world. The Petticoat Policy, the very essence of this book, is not about demanding a seat at the table. Rather, it is about building our table and leading the charge.

For centuries, women have been underestimated, undervalued, and underrepresented in leadership roles. Nevertheless, we have continued to rise, breaking the glass ceiling and shattering stereotypes. The Petticoat Policy is not about fighting against men; it is about fighting for equality, for a world where leadership is not defined by gender but by competence, character, and compassion.

The Petticoat Policy is a clarion call to women across the globe to step up and take charge. It is a call to action, to rise above societal norms and expectations, and to lead with courage and conviction. It is a call to challenge the status quo and redefine what it means to be a leader.

Throughout history, women have proven time and again that they are capable of exceptional leadership. From Joan of Arc to Queen Elizabeth I, from Indira Gandhi to Angela Merkel, women have led nations, led revolutions, and led movements that have changed the world. The Petticoat Policy is a continuation of this legacy, a testament to the power and potential of women in leadership.

Leadership is not about power and dominance. It is about vision, about making a difference, about inspiring others to be the best they can be. The Petticoat Policy is a reminder that women can lead with empathy, integrity, with a sense of purpose that goes beyond personal gain.

The Petticoat Policy is about embracing our strengths, acknowledging our weaknesses, and leading with authenticity. It is about refusing to conform to outdated leadership models and instead, forging our own path. It is about leading with our heads held high, with our hearts open, and with our minds focused on the greater good.

The Petticoat Policy is not just for women. It is for men as well, for it is only when both genders work together when both are given equal opportunities to lead, that we can truly achieve a balanced and equitable society. It is about fostering a culture of respect, of mutual support, of shared responsibility.

The Petticoat Policy is a revolution, a movement, a paradigm shift. It is a beacon of hope for a future where women are not just participants but leaders, where women are not just followers but trailblazers. It is a testament to the strength, resilience, the determination of women across the globe.

Let us rise, let us lead, let us charge forth with the petticoat Policy. Because leadership is not a privilege reserved for a select few. It is a right, a responsibility, a duty that we all share. Let us embrace the petticoat Policy and lead the charge towards a more equitable, more balanced, more inclusive world.

The New Era

The world is at a pivotal point, on the cusp of a revolution that promises to redefine political landscapes, societal norms, and our understanding of power dynamics. It's an era where the once disregarded 'petticoat' is not just an item of clothing, but a symbol of change – a change that is long overdue.

Imagine a world where women's voices are not just heard, but respected and valued. A world where the 'petticoat policy' is not a derogatory term, but a badge of honor. A world where policies and decisions are not dictated by the whims of a single gender, but by the collective wisdom and insights of both men and women.

That is the world we are on the cusp of, the world that is within our grasp if only we dare to reach out and grab it.

The 'petticoat policy' is more than just a concept; it is a call to action. It is a call for women to step into the political arena, to shatter the glass ceiling, and to take their rightful place at the decision-making table. It is a call for men to recognize and appreciate the unique perspectives and contributions that women can bring. And most importantly, it is a call for society to embrace the idea that leadership and power are not the exclusive domains of men, but are traits that can be embodied by anyone, regardless of gender.

But why now? Why is this the 'new era'? The answer is simple. The world is changing, evolving at a rapid pace. From technological advancements to societal shifts, the world as we know it is not the same as it was a decade ago. This evolution necessitates a change in our approach to leadership and policy-making. We can no longer afford to rely on outdated notions of gender roles and power dynamics. The 'petticoat policy' is not just a response to this change, but a proactive step towards shaping a future that is more equitable, more balanced, and more representative.

The 'new era' is not just about women in politics; it's about redefining what politics means. It's about creating an environment where decisions are made based on merit and capability, not on gender. It's about ensuring that the voices of all citizens are heard, not just those of a select few. It's about dismantling the patriarchal structures that have long dictated our political landscape and building a new system that values diversity, inclusivity, and fairness.

So how do we bring about this 'new era'? It starts with each one of us. It starts with recognizing the inherent biases and prejudices that exist within our society and within ourselves. It starts with challenging the status quo and advocating for change. It starts with supporting women in their political endeavors, not as a token gesture, but because they are deserving of these positions. It starts with men stepping up as allies, acknowledging their privilege, and using it to uplift others.

This 'new era' is not a distant dream, but a tangible reality. The 'petticoat policy' is not a passing fad, but a lasting movement. And together, we can make this 'new era' a reality, one where the 'petticoat policy' is not just a policy, but the norm. The time for change is now, and the 'new era' beckons. Are you ready to answer its call?

The Rise of the Female Leader

Women have been at the helm of leadership, making pivotal decisions, and impacting societies for centuries. Yet, it is only in recent times that their roles are being recognized and celebrated. It is essential to understand that the rise of female leaders is not a sudden phenomenon, but a culmination of years of struggle, persistence, and unwavering conviction.

The world of politics, once dominated by men in suits, has seen a significant shift. Women are no longer confined to the backdrop but are stepping into the limelight, leading nations, and driving policy changes. The rise of women leaders represents a change in collective consciousness, a shift towards a more inclusive, balanced, and equitable world.

Women leaders are not just about symbolism or token representation. They bring to the table a unique perspective shaped by their experiences, empathy, and resilience. Their leadership style often mirrors a collaborative and inclusive approach, fostering a sense of community and mutual respect. The world has already witnessed the effectiveness of such a leadership style, especially during crises. The adept handling of the COVID-19 pandemic by women leaders like Jacinda Ardern, Angela Merkel, and Tsai Ing-wen is a testament to their capabilities.

However, the rise of female leaders is not without challenges. The journey to the top is fraught with obstacles, stereotypes, and biases. Women leaders often face intense scrutiny, criticism, and impossibly high standards. The road to leadership is paved with systemic barriers that perpetuate gender disparity. Yet, they persist, undeterred by the challenges, driven by the desire to make a difference.

Moreover, the rise of female leaders is not just about breaking the glass ceiling. It is a catalyst for broader social change. It challenges traditional gender norms, empowers women at the grassroots level, and inspires future generations. It sends a powerful message – that women are not just capable of leading but can do so with grace, strength, and effectiveness.

The rise of female leaders also underscores the importance of representation. Having women in positions of power ensures that women's issues are not just an afterthought but an integral part of policy-making. It ensures that the concerns, aspirations, and rights of half the population are not sidelined but given the importance they deserve.

The world needs more women leaders. Not just because it is the right thing to do, but because it is the smart thing to do. Research indicates that companies with women in leadership positions perform better, have happier employees, and are more innovative. Similarly, countries led by women tend to have better social indicators, lower corruption, and higher economic growth.

Therefore, the rise of female leaders is not just a trend but a necessity. It is not just about gender equality but about harnessing the full potential of humanity. It is not just about women but about creating a better, more equitable, and just world for everyone.

The rise of female leaders is not a threat but a promise – a promise of a world where leadership is not defined by gender but by competence, integrity, and vision. So, let us celebrate the rise of female leaders, let us support them, learn from them, and most importantly, let us strive to be them.

IN THE WORKPLACE

Battling Bias

In the realm of societal norms and gender roles, a significant hurdle that must be surmounted is the ingrained bias that often goes unnoticed. The 'petticoat policy' is a stark representation of the bias that has been deeply embedded in our society. It is a term coined to represent the skewed perception that women are only fit for domestic roles, their abilities and potential confined to the supposed safety of the Petticoat. This bias is not only harmful but also grossly inaccurate, and it is high time we started addressing it.

Gender bias, particularly against women, has been prevalent for centuries. It is a systemic issue that has permeated every aspect of our lives, from the workplace to the home, from politics to sports. Women have been marginalized, their voices silenced, their capabilities underestimated, and their potential untapped. They have been stigmatized and stereotyped, confined to the narrow roles that society has deemed 'appropriate' for them. This is the Petticoat policy, a policy that has been enforced, either consciously or unconsciously, by a male-dominated society.

However, it is crucial to remember that this bias is not an inherent trait of human nature but a social construct that has been perpetuated over time. It is a learned behavior, which means it can be unlearned. It is not an irreversible condition but a mutable one. It is not a permanent fixture of our society but a temporary aberration that can be rectified.

The key to battling this bias lies in awareness and education. We must first recognize the existence of this bias before we can begin to dismantle it. We must acknowledge the fact that women are not inherently inferior or incapable, but have been conditioned to believe so by a society that values masculinity over femininity. We must educate ourselves and others about the detrimental effects of this bias, not only on women but also on society as a whole.

In the quest to eradicate this bias, it is important to challenge the traditional gender roles and stereotypes that have been ingrained in our minds. We must encourage women to step out of the confines of the Petticoat and explore their potential in every sphere of life. We must provide them with the same opportunities and resources that are readily available to men. We must treat them as equals, not as inferiors or objects of pity.

Moreover, men must also play an active role in this battle against bias. They must recognize their privilege and use it to uplift and empower women, rather than oppress and undermine them. They must acknowledge the fact that women are not threats but allies, not competitors but collaborators, not burdens but assets.

The fight against bias is not a women's issue but a human issue. It is not a fight against men but a fight for equality and justice. It is not a fight for superiority but a fight for parity. It is not a fight to tear down men but a fight to build up women. It is a fight that requires the collective efforts of all members of society, regardless of their gender.

In the grand scheme of things, the Petticoat policy is not just a policy but a mindset, a mindset that needs to be changed. The battle against bias is not just a battle but a revolution, a revolution that needs to be ignited. And the time to ignite that revolution is now.

Equal Pay, Equal Work

In the realm of gender equality, it is a well-established fact that women have been disadvantaged when it comes to remuneration for their work. The notion of 'petticoat policy' has been used as a tool to relegate women to lesser paying roles, fostering a culture of gender disparity that is nothing short of unacceptable. It is high time that we challenge the status quo and advocate for the principle of 'equal pay for equal work'.

The crux of the matter is simple. If a woman performs the same tasks with the same degree of competence as her male counterpart, it is only fair that she should receive the same remuneration. There is no logical or ethical reasoning that justifies women being paid less for the same work. It is a glaring example of gender discrimination that needs to be addressed and rectified.

The argument for 'equal pay for equal work' is not just about fairness, it is about respect. It sends a clear message that a woman's work is just as valuable and significant as a man's. It underlines the fact that women are not lesser beings, but equal contributors in every field of work. It is a testament to their skills, capabilities, and contributions, recognizing them as vital cogs in the machinery of progress.

Moreover, it is not just about individual respect and dignity, but also about the broader societal implications. When we ensure equal pay for equal work, we are fostering a society where gender does not determine one's worth. It creates a culture of respect, appreciation, and equality that transcends the workplace and permeates every aspect of our lives.

The benefits of 'equal pay for equal work' are not limited to the individual or societal level. From an economic perspective, it makes perfect sense. When women are paid equally, their purchasing power increases, which in turn stimulates the economy. It also encourages more women to join the workforce, thereby increasing the pool of talent and leading to overall economic growth.

Despite these compelling arguments, the reality is that we still have a long way to go. The gender pay gap persists, and it is our collective responsibility to bridge it. It requires concerted efforts from all stakeholders, including governments, corporations, and individuals. Legislation needs to be enacted and enforced, corporate policies need to be revised, and societal attitudes need to change.

It is also crucial to dispel the misconceptions surrounding 'equal pay for equal work'. It is not about 'favoring' women or 'penalizing' men. It is about rectifying a historical wrong and ensuring a level playing field for all. It is about acknowledging that gender should not be a determinant of one's worth or remuneration.

The 'petticoat policy' has had its day. It is time to consign it to the annals of history where it belongs. The future must be one of equality, respect, and fairness. 'Equal pay for equal work' is not just a slogan, it is a principle that we need to uphold and champion. It is an idea whose time has come, a cause that we must all rally behind. Because in the final analysis, a society that values all its members equally is a society that truly thrives.

The Motherhood Penalty

In a society that prides itself on equality and progress, it is disheartening to note that a significant bias still exists against working mothers. This bias, often referred to as the 'Motherhood Penalty', is a stark example of the systemic gender inequality that persists in our workplaces. It is a disturbing reality that needs to be urgently addressed and rectified.

The Motherhood Penalty is a term that encapsulates the myriad of prejudices and disadvantages faced by working mothers. These manifest in various forms including lower wages, fewer opportunities for advancement, and a general lack of support and understanding from employers and colleagues. Despite the fact that women have made significant strides in the workforce, the advent of motherhood seems to set them back, creating a disturbing paradox.

The statistics are alarming. According to a study by the National Women's Law Center, for every dollar a man earns, a mother earns just 71 cents. This pays gap widens with the number of children a woman has. Furthermore, women with children are less likely to be hired and, if they are, they are often offered lower salaries compared to their childless counterparts.

We must question why, in the 21st century, motherhood is still seen as a liability rather than an asset. Why is it that a woman's dedication to her family is perceived as a sign of decreased commitment to her career? Why is it that employers fail to see the transferable skills that motherhood can bring to the workplace - skills such as multitasking, time management, problem-solving, and crisis management?

It is time we debunked the myth that mothers cannot be as committed, efficient or productive as their childless peers. It is time we recognized and valued the incredible balancing act that working mothers perform every day. They juggle multiple roles and responsibilities without compromising on either front, displaying a level of dedication, resilience, and efficiency that is nothing short of remarkable.

We must also acknowledge that the Motherhood Penalty is not just a women's issue, it is a societal issue. It affects families, economies, and societies at large. When mothers earn less, families have less. When families have less, economies suffer. When economies suffer, societies stagnate.

To address this issue, we must advocate for policies that support working mothers such as flexible working hours, paid maternity leave, affordable childcare, and equal pay. Employers need to be educated about the Motherhood Penalty and encouraged to implement family-friendly policies. It is also crucial to challenge societal attitudes and stereotypes about working mothers.

The Motherhood Penalty is a stark reminder of the gender inequality that still exists in our society. But it is also a call to action. A call to challenge the status quo, to fight for equality, and to create a world where motherhood is not a penalty but a celebration. A world where women are not penalized for their choice to be both mothers and professionals. A world where the potential of every woman is recognized and valued, regardless of her maternal status.

We owe it to ourselves, and to future generations, to address the Motherhood Penalty. It's high time we acknowledged that motherhood is not a liability, but a strength. It's high time we stopped penalizing mothers and started valuing them for the incredible individuals they are. Because when mothers thrive, we all thrive.

The Corner Office

The corner office, that symbol of power and prestige, is often perceived as the ultimate professional goal, a mark of having 'made it'. It is here that the weighty decisions are made, the future of the company is shaped, and the corporate world is led. But who sits in this coveted space? Who wields this tremendous power? Is it not time that we see more diversity in the corner office, more women at the helm of our companies?

The world of business, like many other fields, has long been dominated by men. The corner office has traditionally been a male preserve, a place where women were rarely seen. But times are changing. We are in the 21st century, an era of progress and equality. Women are breaking down barriers, shattering glass ceilings and proving that they are just as capable, if not more so, as their male counterparts.

Yet, despite this progress, there remains a glaring gender imbalance in the corner office. Women are still woefully underrepresented in the highest echelons of corporate power. This is not just a matter of fairness or equality. It's a matter of business sense.

Multiple studies have shown that companies with women in leadership positions perform better, are more profitable, and have higher employee satisfaction rates. Diverse leadership teams bring different perspectives, ideas and solutions to the table, leading to better decision making and innovation.

Think about it. Women make up half of the world's population, and they control a significant amount of purchasing power. They are consumers, clients, and employees. Doesn't it make sense, then, that they should also be leaders, decision-makers and influencers?

The corner office should not be a space that is reserved for one gender. It should be a space where talent, skill, and leadership are valued, regardless of whether they come in a suit or aPettycoat. Women have proven time and again that they are more than capable of leading, of making tough decisions, of guiding companies to success.

It's time to change our perception of the corner office. It's time to welcome more women into this space, to value their contributions, their ideas, and their leadership. We need to get rid of outdated notions of gender roles and embrace the idea that anyone, regardless of gender, can lead.

The corner office should not be a symbol of male power, but a symbol of leadership, of success, of achievement. And women, just as much as men, deserve to sit in that chair, to look out of that window, to lead from that room.

Let's change the narrative. Let's make the corner office a place where everyone, regardless of gender, can aspire to be. Let's make it a place where women's voices are heard, where their ideas are valued, and where their leadership is celebrated.

Let's make the corner office a place of equality, of opportunity, of progress. Because when women succeed, we all succeed. When women lead, we all benefit. It's not just good for women, it's good for business, it's good for society, it's good for us all.

So, here's to the women in the corner office, and to those who aspire to be there. Your time is now. Your place is here. You belong in the corner office. Because the corner office needs you.

IN POLITICS

The Glass Cliff

In the realm of gender politics and corporate leadership, a fascinating phenomenon has emerged, dubbed the 'Glass Cliff.' This metaphorical precipice represents the precarious positions women often find themselves in when they break through the metaphorical 'glass ceiling' to reach high-ranking positions. It is a concept that cannot be ignored in our exploration of the Petticoat policy.

Women, when they do ascend to positions of power, often find themselves in precarious, high-risk situations. They are more likely to be appointed to leadership roles in times of crisis or uncertainty, when the chance of failure is significantly higher. This is the essence of the Glass Cliff – a perilous edge that many women leaders unwittingly stand upon, teetering on the brink of a precipitous fall.

Evidence of the Glass Cliff can be seen across various sectors, from politics to business, where women are often appointed in times of turmoil. They are brought in to clean up messes they didn't create, to steer sinking ships they didn't scuttle, and to restore faith in systems they didn't erode. This is not a coincidence. It is a pattern, a policy of sorts, that needs to be examined and challenged.

The Glass Cliff is a dangerous double-edged sword. On one hand, it provides women with opportunities to rise to positions of power that might otherwise remain inaccessible. On the other hand, it sets them up for potential failure, and the subsequent blame that comes with it. This can perpetuate harmful stereotypes about women's leadership abilities, creating a cycle that is difficult to break.

Moreover, the Glass Cliff is indicative of a deeper issue. It suggests that women's leadership is valued only when things are going wrong, and not in times of stability or success. This is a clear reflection of the gender bias that still pervades our society, where women are expected to nurture and heal, rather than lead and innovate.

The Glass Cliff is not just a challenge for women, it is a societal issue. It tells us something about how we perceive and value leadership. It is a reminder that breaking the glass ceiling is not enough; the path to true gender equality is fraught with hidden obstacles. To overcome them, we must acknowledge their existence and actively work to dismantle them.

We must question why women are often handed the reins in times of crisis. We must challenge the narrative that women are merely crisis managers rather than effective leaders. It is time to shatter the Glass Cliff, to ensure that women are given the same opportunities to lead, not just when times are tough, but when the sun is shining too.

We cannot afford to be complacent. The Glass Cliff is a subtle yet potent barrier to gender equality. By acknowledging and addressing it, we can create a more equitable, inclusive world where women's leadership is not just valued in times of crisis, but at all times. Let us not allow the Glass Cliff to be another glass ceiling for women. Instead, let it be a stepping stone to a higher plane of equality and fairness. This is the true essence of the Petticoat policy.

The Seat at the Table

Ladies and gentlemen, it is high time we shift our perspective and acknowledge the glaring truth - there is an evident lack of female representation in the highest echelons of power. This is not a mere observation, but a pressing concern that we must address. The 'petty coat policy' as we call it, is not about giving undue advantage to women. It is about creating an even playing field, a space where women can contribute their unique perspectives and ideas.

Consider this, only a fraction of our policy-making bodies worldwide comprises women. This is not due to a lack of capable women, but rather the result of deep-seated prejudices and biases. It is crucial to understand that denying women their rightful place in these arenas is not only unfair but also detrimental to our collective growth.

In the realm of decision-making, diverse perspectives lead to more comprehensive and effective solutions. When women are included in these processes, they bring a fresh viewpoint, often shedding light on issues that may otherwise be overlooked. They bring empathy, resilience, and a unique understanding of societal dynamics, which can significantly enhance policy outcomes.

Now, imagine a world where women are equally represented in the corridors of power. A world where decisions about women are not made without women. A world where the 'petty coat policy' is not the exception but the norm. This is not an unattainable utopia but a very achievable reality.

However, achieving this reality requires concerted effort and action. We need to dismantle the barriers that hinder women's progress and create an environment that encourages their participation. This begins with changing our mindsets. We need to let go of outdated stereotypes that confine women to certain roles and responsibilities.

Moreover, we need to invest in women's education and leadership development. Empowering women with knowledge and skills is the first step towards their active involvement in decision-making. We must also ensure that women are given equal opportunities and are evaluated based on their merit and not their gender.

Furthermore, we need to implement policies that protect women's rights and promote their participation. These policies should address issues such as gender pay gap, sexual harassment, and discrimination. They should also provide provisions for maternity leave and childcare, thus enabling women to balance their professional and personal lives.

It is also essential to have role models - women who have broken the glass ceiling and made their mark. Their stories can inspire and motivate other women to strive for leadership roles.

The 'petty coat policy' is not about favoring women over men. It is about acknowledging and respecting women's capabilities. It is about creating a society where decisions are made by a diverse group of individuals who represent all segments of the population.

So, let's take a step towards this change. Let's ensure that women have a seat at the table, not as a token gesture, but as a testament to their abilities and contributions. Let's make the 'petty coat policy' a reality. Because when women succeed, we all succeed.

The Power of the Vote

In the grand scheme of democracy, the individual vote is a powerful tool. It's a beacon of hope, a symbol of change, and an emblem of freedom. It's the power of the vote that shapes the political landscape, directs the course of nations, and determines the fate of societies. It's more than just a simple act of casting a ballot; it's a manifestation of the collective will of the people.

Consider this: every major political change in history has been brought about by the power of the vote. From the abolition of slavery to the suffrage movement, from civil rights to gender equality, the vote has always been at the heart of social transformation. It's the most effective way for ordinary citizens to influence government policies and hold their leaders accountable.

The power of the vote is not just about choosing who will lead us, but also about deciding on crucial issues that affect our daily lives. From education and healthcare to economy and environment, voting gives us a say in shaping the policies that govern these areas. It's an opportunity for us to voice our opinions, express our concerns, and advocate for the changes we want to see in our society.

Yet, the power of the vote is often underestimated and underutilized. Many people feel that their single vote doesn't make a difference, that it's a drop in the ocean. But history has proven otherwise. There have been numerous instances where a single vote has swung the outcome of an election, changed the course of a policy, or even altered the direction of a nation.

The power of the vote becomes even more important when it comes to women's rights and gender equality. The vote is not just a right; it's a tool for empowerment. It gives women the power to influence decisions that affect their lives, their families, and their communities. It's a means to fight against discrimination, inequality, and injustice.

Women's vote has been instrumental in bringing about significant changes in society. From advocating for equal pay to fighting against domestic violence, from promoting girls' education to demanding reproductive rights, women have used their vote to challenge the status quo and drive social progress.

However, the fight is far from over. Even today, there are countless women around the world who are denied their right to vote, who are silenced by societal norms and cultural biases. It's our responsibility to ensure that every woman has the freedom to exercise her right to vote, to make her voice heard, and to contribute to the democratic process.

The power of the vote is not just about the ability to elect leaders or decide on policies. It's about the power to shape our own destiny, to create a society that reflects our values and aspirations. It's about using our collective power to bring about change, to make a difference, and to create a better world.

So, let's not take our right to vote for granted. Let's use it wisely, responsibly, and passionately. Let's harness the power of the vote to create a society that respects and values the rights of all its citizens, regardless of their gender, race, or ethnicity. Because in the end, it's not just about the power of the vote; it's about the power of the people.

The Future is Equal

As we turn the pages of history, we find a consistent pattern of women being relegated to the sidelines, their contributions often overlooked or undervalued. This, however, is an old narrative and the world is witnessing a paradigm shift. The Petty coat Policy is not just about recognizing and appreciating the efforts of women, but it is also about envisioning a future where equality is not just a notion but a reality.

Imagine a world where opportunities are not divided based on gender. Picture a society where men and women work side by side, not just in homes, but also in offices, laboratories, government, and more. This is not a utopian dream, but a future that is within our reach, a future that is equal.

The world is evolving, and women are at the forefront of this change. They are breaking barriers, shattering glass ceilings, and making their mark across all sectors. This is not a wave that will ebb; it is a tide that is rising. The future is not about men versus women; it is about men and women together, building a world that is equitable and just.

Change, however, is not always easy. It requires a shift in mindset, a change in attitudes, and a commitment to fairness. It requires us to challenge our prejudices and question our biases. It requires us to acknowledge that women are not just capable, but they are also deserving of every opportunity that men are afforded.

The future is equal, but it is not just about equality in opportunities; it is also about equality in recognition. It is about acknowledging the contributions of women, not just in the domestic sphere, but also in the professional arena. It is about recognizing that the success of a society is not just built on the shoulders of men, but also on the efforts and sacrifices of women.

The future is equal, but it is not just about women. It is about creating a society where every individual, regardless of their gender, has the opportunity to thrive. It is about ensuring that every person is judged not based on their gender, but on their abilities, their efforts, and their contributions.

The Petty coat Policy is not just a book; it is a manifesto for change, a call to action. It is a plea to every individual to play their part in creating a future that is equal. It is a request to every organization, every government, and every society to make equality not just a priority, but a reality.

The future is equal, but the journey towards this future is not easy. It requires courage, it requires conviction, and it requires commitment. It requires us to stand up against inequality, to speak up against injustice, and to fight for what is right.

The future is equal, and it is within our reach. We have the power to change the narrative, to rewrite the story. We have the power to create a future that is not just equal, but also fair, just, and inclusive. The future is equal, and it starts with us.

IN EDUCATION

The Right to Learn

Imagine a world where the right to education isn't a privilege but a fundamental right; where every child, regardless of their gender, race, or socioeconomic status, has the opportunity to learn, grow, and reach their full potential. That's the world we should be striving for, yet sadly, it is not the world we live in today. The barriers to education are many, but none more so than the misguided and antiquated notion that some individuals, particularly women, are less deserving of knowledge than others. This is the petty coat policy at play, a policy that is not just unfair but fundamentally wrong.

Education is not a luxury; it's a basic human right that should be accessible to all. It's the driving force behind individual growth, societal innovation, and global progress. It's the tool that empowers us to question, to challenge, and to change. Denying someone the right to education is equivalent to denying them the right to thrive.

It's time to challenge the petty coat policy. It's time to recognize that a person's worth is not defined by their gender, but by their potential, their dreams, and their capacity to contribute meaningfully to society. Let's not forget that the world's most successful societies are those that have embraced equality in education. They have understood that to truly progress, we must educate all, not just a select few.

We must also understand that the right to learn is not just about academic education. It's about the right to knowledge and understanding in all its forms. It's about the right to learn about oneself and the world around us. It's about the right to develop critical thinking skills, to question, and to challenge.

The petty coat policy is not just a hindrance to individual growth, but to societal progress as well. When we deny women the right to learn, we are denying society the benefit of their potential contributions. We are stifling innovation, creativity, and progress.

Let's look at the facts. Studies have shown that when women are educated, societies thrive. Educated women are more likely to participate in the workforce, earn higher incomes, and support healthier and more educated families. They are more likely to stand up for their rights and challenge societal norms that hold them back.

The petty coat policy is not just unjust, it's counterproductive. It's a policy that limits, rather than encourages, potential. It's a policy that hinders, rather than fosters, progress. It's a policy that we must challenge and overcome.

The fight against the petty coat policy is not just a fight for women's rights, but a fight for human rights. It's a fight for equality, for progress, and for a better world. It's a fight that we must all participate in, for the sake of our future and the future of generations to come.

The right to learn is not a privilege, it's a right. It's a right that we must uphold, protect, and champion. It's a right that we must fight for, not just for ourselves, but for everyone. Because the right to learn is the right to thrive, and that is a right that should never be denied.

Battling Stereotypes

In a world still dominated by male perspectives, women continue to face a daunting array of stereotypes that undermine their abilities and contributions. These stereotypes persist, often subtly, in our everyday interactions, media narratives, and institutional practices. They are not only detrimental to women's self-esteem and career progression but also hinder societal development as a whole by stiffening the untapped potential of half of the world's population.

The first step in combating these stereotypes is to acknowledge their existence. It is important to recognize that stereotypes are not just harmless jokes or casual comments but deeply ingrained societal norms that shape our perceptions and behaviors. They are pervasive and insidious, often influencing our decisions unconsciously. Denial or dismissal of their existence only perpetuates their harmful effects.

Once we acknowledge these stereotypes, we must actively challenge them. We must question the traditional narratives that confine women to certain roles and fields. Why should women be expected to be nurturing and empathetic, but not assertive or ambitious? Why should women be relegated to the 'soft' fields of humanities and social sciences, but not the 'hard' fields of science, technology, engineering, and mathematics? These stereotypes not only limit women's choices and opportunities but also devalue the skills and contributions associated with femininity.

Challenging these stereotypes requires us to rethink our language and imagery. The words and images we use have profound implications for how we perceive and treat women. For instance, describing women as 'bossy' or 'emotional' reinforces the stereotype that women are not suited for leadership roles. Similarly, portraying women as passive or objectified in media reinforces the stereotype that women are not agents of their own lives. We must strive for more balanced and diverse representations of women in all aspects of life.

Moreover, we must promote positive role models who defy these stereotypes. Role models are powerful tools for social change as they provide tangible proof that stereotypes are not truths. They inspire and empower women to break free from societal expectations and forge their own paths. We must celebrate women who excel in traditionally male-dominated fields, women who balance work and family life, and women who challenge the status quo in their unique ways.

Additionally, we must foster inclusive and equitable environments that value diversity and inclusivity. Stereotypes thrive in homogeneous environments where the 'other' is perceived as different and inferior. By creating spaces where diverse voices and perspectives are heard and valued, we can challenge the assumptions and biases that underpin stereotypes.

Lastly, we must remember that battling stereotypes is not just a women's issue. It is a societal issue that requires everyone's involvement. Men, too, are constrained by gender stereotypes that dictate how they should behave and what they should aspire to. By challenging these stereotypes, we can create a more equitable and inclusive society where everyone is free to be themselves and realize their full potential.

In this battle against stereotypes, every small step counts. Every time we question a stereotype, every time we challenge a biased narrative, every time we celebrate a woman's achievement, we are contributing to a larger movement for gender equality. Let's not underestimate the power of our collective actions. Together, we can break down the barriers of stereotypes and build a more equitable and inclusive society.

The Fight for Fairness

As we delve deeper into the realms of petty coat policy, it is essential to address the elephant in the room – the unrelenting struggle for equality. The fight for fairness is not a new issue; it has been a pivotal aspect of human history, deeply entrenched in our societies since time immemorial. But what does fairness mean in the context of petty coat policy? It signifies the quest for equal representation, respect, and opportunities for women in the political arena.

Despite the significant strides we have made in the 21st century, the scales of justice remain tipped in favor of the patriarchal order, especially in politics. Women, despite their merit and capabilities, are often overlooked, underrepresented, or blatantly dismissed. This disparity is not just an attack on the individual rights of women, but it also robs our societies of the diverse perspectives and innovative ideas that women bring to the table.

Imagine a world where women have equal representation in the political sphere. A world where the petty coat policy is not just a concept, but a reality. This is not a utopian dream, but a plausible reality that we can achieve if we collectively fight for fairness.

The fight for fairness is not a battle against men, but against an outdated system that perpetuates gender inequality. It is a fight against the stereotypical notions that confine women to the private sphere and perceive them as unfit for politics. It is a fight against the societal structures that favor the privileged few and perpetuate the glass ceiling.

The fight for fairness is not just about achieving numerical equality but substantive equality. It is about ensuring that women have the same opportunities as their male counterparts to influence political decisions. It is about making sure that women's voices are heard, their concerns addressed, and their contributions acknowledged.

How do we fight for fairness? We start by challenging the status quo. We question the norms that have been normalized, the stereotypes that have been internalized, and the biases that have been institutionalized. We must strive to create an inclusive political environment that respects and values the contributions of women.

We must also work towards developing policies that facilitate women's participation in politics. This could include measures like affirmative action, gender quotas, and capacity-building programs for women. However, these policies must not be seen as tokenistic gestures, but as genuine efforts to rectify the systemic barriers that hinder women's political participation.

Moreover, we must also focus on educating and empowering women. We need to instill in them the confidence to break the shackles of gender norms and to assert their rightful place in the political sphere. We must encourage them to raise their voices against injustice, to question authority, and to fight for their rights.

The fight for fairness is a daunting task. It requires courage, resilience, and determination. It requires us to challenge deeply ingrained prejudices and to question entrenched power structures. But it is a fight worth fighting, for it promises a world where the petty coat policy is not just a concept, but a reality. A world where women are not just spectators, but active participants in the political arena. A world where fairness reigns supreme, and equality is not just an ideal, but a lived reality.

Let us, therefore, stand united in this fight for fairness. Let us challenge the unfair practices, break the glass ceilings, and shatter the patriarchal structures. Let us strive to create a world where the petty coat policy is not just an aspiration, but a manifestation of our collective will to ensure equality and justice for all.

The Power of Knowledge

In the realm of the Petticoat policy, understanding and harnessing the power of knowledge is paramount. We live in a world where information is readily available, yet the ability to discern, dissect, and apply this knowledge effectively is a skill that is not as widespread. Knowledge is not merely the possession of information; it is the aptitude to employ this information to influence, to create change, and to progress.

The potency of knowledge is undeniable. It is the key that unlocks opportunities, fosters growth, and precipitates transformation. The more knowledge you have, the more tools you possess to navigate the complexities of life. It is an empowering entity that cultivates confidence, fosters independence, and propels advancement. It is a formidable weapon against ignorance, prejudice, and inequality.

Within the framework of the Petticoat policy, knowledge is the cornerstone of empowerment. It is the force that shatters the glass ceiling, the impetus that propels women forward in a world that often seeks to hold them back. It is the catalyst for change, the fuel for progress, and the means to challenge and transform the status quo.

Knowledge is not a static entity; it is dynamic and constantly evolving. It demands curiosity, openness, and a willingness to learn. It requires us to question, to probe, and to challenge the accepted norms and paradigms. It is not enough to be a passive recipient of information. We must be active participants in the process of learning, continually seeking out new information, perspectives, and insights.

In the context of the Petticoat policy, this means challenging the traditional narratives and stereotypes that have long defined and confined women. It means seeking out and amplifying the voices and experiences of women who have been marginalized, overlooked, and silenced. It means leveraging our collective knowledge to dismantle the barriers that impede women's progress and to construct a world that is inclusive, equitable, and just.

Knowledge is a powerful tool, but it is only as effective as our ability to wield it. It is not enough to simply possess knowledge; we must also have the courage to use it. This means speaking out against injustice, challenging the status quo, and advocating for change. It means using our knowledge to inform, to enlighten, and to inspire.

The power of knowledge is not a luxury; it is a necessity. It is the foundation upon which we build our lives, our societies, and our world. It is the driving force behind progress, the catalyst for change, and the key to empowerment. It is a weapon against ignorance, a tool for advancement, and a beacon of hope in a world that often seems dark.

We must never underestimate the power of knowledge. It is our greatest ally in the pursuit of equality, justice, and progress. It is the heartbeat of the Petticoat policy, the lifeblood of our movement, and the soul of our struggle. It is the power that propels us forward, the force that drives us, and the spark that ignites our passion.

The power of knowledge is not just about learning; it is about understanding. It is about seeing the world through a different lens, challenging our preconceptions, and redefining our perspectives. It is about acknowledging our past, confronting our present, and shaping our future. It is about empowering ourselves and empowering others. It is about harnessing the power of knowledge to change the world.

IN SOCIETY

The Social Script

From the moment of birth, society hands us a script. This script, a preconceived notion of how we should behave, think, and interact with the world around us, is heavily influenced by our gender. In this context, we'll delve into the idea of the 'petticoat policy', a term used to describe the subtle and often unnoticed ways in which society controls, directs, and influences women's behavior.

The character of the 'good girl' is a perfect example of the social script. She is obedient, polite, and always puts others' needs before her own. She never raises her voice, always agreeing with the majority, even if it contradicts her personal beliefs. This script is so deeply ingrained in our psyche that we often fail to recognize it. We accept it as a norm, and women who deviate from this script are often criticized, ostracized, or labeled as 'difficult'.

Consider the language we use. The term 'bossy' is often used to describe assertive women, while their male counterparts are lauded for their 'leadership' skills. This is not a mere play of words. It's a subtle way of enforcing the social script, of reminding women of their 'place'.

The script doesn't stop at behavioral norms. It extends to personal and professional choices as well. Women are expected to prioritize family over career, to be caregivers rather than providers. They are often questioned and judged for their choices, be it the decision to remain single, to not have children, or to pursue a demanding career.

The social script is not just about controlling women's behavior. It is also about maintaining the status quo, about preserving the existing power structures. It is about ensuring that women remain in their 'designated' roles, that they do not challenge the traditional norms and values.

But here's the thing. This social script, as pervasive and powerful as it may seem, is not set in stone. It can be rewritten. And the first step to doing that is recognizing its existence. It is about understanding that these scripts are not inherent truths, but social constructs. It's about challenging these norms, about questioning the stereotypes, about breaking the mold.

To rewrite the script, we need to start by acknowledging the diversity and complexity of women's experiences. We need to understand that there is no 'one size fits all' approach to womanhood, that women are not a monolithic group. We need to celebrate women's individuality, their strengths, their ambitions, and their dreams.

We need to create a society where women are not judged for their choices, where they are not expected to conform to a certain ideal. A society where women are not just allowed, but encouraged to be themselves.

The 'petticoat policy' is not just about women. It's about all of us. It's about creating a more equitable, more inclusive society. It's about recognizing and challenging the social scripts that limit us, that prevent us from realizing our full potential. And it starts with us. We are the authors of our own scripts. Let's make them count.

Breaking the Mould

In a world where patriarchal norms have dominated for centuries, it's time to redefine the rules and break the mould. The 'petticoat policy' isn't about replacing one gender with another in the power dynamics. Instead, it's about embracing the values of inclusivity, diversity, and equality. It's about shifting the paradigm to a space where the feminine and the masculine coexist and complement each other in the policy-making process.

We need to challenge the status quo and shatter the glass ceilings that have been hindering women from reaching their full potential. This is not just about women's rights. It's about human rights. It's about the right to equal opportunities and fair treatment regardless of one's gender. It's about creating a world where your gender doesn't determine your worth or limit your opportunities.

The 'petticoat policy' is not a radical feminist agenda. It's a call to action for everyone - men and women alike - to be part of the change. It's a call to action to question, to challenge, and to change the traditional norms that have been inhibiting progress. It's a call to action to create a world where everyone has the freedom to be who they are, to do what they love, and to achieve what they aspire for, without any gender-based limitations.

The 'petticoat policy' is not about creating a matriarchal society. It's about creating a gender-balanced society. It's about creating a world where leadership is not associated with masculinity, and compassion is not associated with femininity. It's about creating a world where men and women are appreciated for their unique qualities and contributions, and not judged based on their gender.

The 'petticoat policy' is not about women taking over. It's about women taking their rightful place. It's about acknowledging the role of women in shaping our society and our future. It's about recognizing the power of the feminine and leveraging it for the betterment of our world.

The 'petticoat policy' is not about dividing us. It's about uniting us. It's about recognizing that our differences make us stronger. It's about celebrating our diversity and harnessing it for our collective progress.

The 'petticoat policy' is not about the battle of the sexes. It's about the harmony of the sexes. It's about creating a world where men and women work together, hand in hand, towards a common goal. It's about creating a world where the success of one is the success of all.

The 'petticoat policy' is not about demanding special privileges for women. It's about demanding equal rights and opportunities for all. It's about creating a world where everyone is judged based on their abilities and contributions, and not their gender.

The 'petticoat policy' is not about weakening men. It's about empowering everyone. It's about creating a world where everyone has the power to shape their destiny, regardless of their gender.

The 'petticoat policy' is not just a policy. It's a revolution. It's a movement towards a more inclusive, diverse, and equitable world. It's a movement towards a world where everyone is valued, respected, and empowered. It's a movement towards a better future for all. So, let's break the mould. Let's embrace the 'petticoat policy'.

The Power of Perception

In our world, perception is a powerful tool. It shapes our understanding and interpretation of reality, influencing our decisions and actions. In the context of the 'petticoat policy', perception plays a pivotal role. It can either reinforce the status quo or challenge it, opening doors for a new era of gender equality.

We often hear the phrase 'perception is reality'. This statement holds true when discussing the 'petticoat policy'. The way society perceives women and their roles profoundly impacts women's opportunities and experiences. If the perception is that women are not capable or suitable for certain roles, it becomes a self-fulfilling prophecy. Women are then less likely to be considered for these roles, and the cycle continues, perpetuating gender inequality.

However, the power of perception can also be harnessed for positive change. If we perceive women as competent and capable leaders, this can lead to an increase in women's representation in positions of power. Perception is not a static concept; it is fluid and can be changed. We all have the capacity to challenge and reshape our perceptions, and this is where the real power lies.

Consider a world where the 'petticoat policy' is not merely an exception but the norm. This shift would require a radical change in perception. A society that perceives women as equal contributors and leaders in all fields would be one that truly embraces the 'petticoat policy'. This is not a fantastical, utopian vision but a realistic goal that is attainable with a shift in perception.

The power of perception extends beyond individual beliefs; it influences social structures and policy decisions. Legislation and policies that promote gender equality often stem from a shift in societal perception. When we begin to perceive women as equally capable and deserving of leadership roles, it becomes a societal expectation that policies should reflect this belief.

Yet, changing perception is no easy task. It requires a concerted effort from all members of society. Challenging deeply ingrained beliefs and stereotypes about gender roles can be uncomfortable, but it is a necessary step towards achieving gender equality.

The 'petticoat policy' is not simply about allowing women to hold positions of power. It's about changing the perception of women and their capabilities. It's about breaking down the barriers that prevent women from reaching their full potential.

Perception holds the key to unlocking a world where the 'petticoat policy' is the standard, not the exception. It's about time we recognize and harness this power. The power to perceive women as they truly are - competent, capable, and deserving of equal opportunities.

The 'petticoat policy' challenges us to examine our perceptions. It encourages us to question our beliefs and attitudes towards women in leadership roles. It urges us to consider the possibility that our perceptions may be flawed, and it invites us to change them.

Let's wield the power of perception to challenge the status quo and usher in a new era of gender equality. The 'petticoat policy' is not just a policy; it's a movement, a call to action, a challenge to our perceptions. Let's answer this call and create a world where every woman has the opportunity to lead.

The Fight for Respect

In a world dominated by patriarchal norms and expectations, the struggle for recognition and respect is a constant uphill battle for women. The Petticoat may be seen as a symbol of femininity, yet it also embodies the fight for equality, for respect, and for recognition. It is a fight that is as relevant today as it was a century ago, and it is a fight that is far from over.

Women have always been expected to conform to societal norms that limit their potential. From being confined to the domestic sphere to being denied the right to vote or own property, women have been systematically marginalized and denied their rightful place in society. But the fight for respect is not just about breaking down walls; it is also about building bridges. It is about changing attitudes and challenging stereotypes. It is about empowering women to stand up for their rights and to assert their individuality.

The Petticoat, often seen as a symbol of submissiveness and subservience, has been transformed into a symbol of resistance and empowerment. It is a powerful reminder of the struggles that women have faced and continue to face in their quest for equality. But it is also a testament to their strength, their resilience, and their determination to fight for their rights.

The fight for respect is not just about gaining recognition in society; it is also about gaining respect within oneself. It is about recognizing one's worth and refusing to settle for less than one deserves. It is about having the courage to stand up for one's beliefs and to make one's voice heard. It is about refusing to be silenced or sidelined, and instead, demanding to be seen and heard.

The fight for respect is a collective struggle that encompasses all women, regardless of their race, religion, or social status. It is a fight that transcends borders and cultures, and it is a fight that requires solidarity and unity. It is a fight that demands action, not just words.

The Petticoat policy is not just a policy; it is a movement. It is a call to action for all women to rise up and demand their rightful place in society. It is a call to challenge the status quo and to break free from the chains of patriarchy. It is a call to fight for respect, for equality, and for justice.

The fight for respect is a fight that we must all undertake. It is a fight that requires courage, determination, and resilience. But it is a fight that we can win. With the Petticoat as our symbol, we can stand tall and proud, knowing that we are fighting for a cause that is just and right. We can stand strong, knowing that we are not alone, and that we are part of a movement that is bigger than ourselves. We can stand together, knowing that we are making a difference, and that we are paving the way for future generations.

The fight for respect is a fight that we cannot afford to lose. For the sake of our daughters, our granddaughters, and all the women who will come after us, we must continue to fight. We must continue to demand respect, not just for ourselves, but for all women. And we must continue to wear our Petticoats with pride, knowing that they are not just a symbol of femininity, but a symbol of strength, resilience, and determination.

IN THE MEDIA

The Portrayal of Women

Within the pages of 'Petticoat Policy', we delve into the fascinating world of women's representation, a topic that has been a point of contention for centuries. This subchapter is an exploration of the portrayal of women, a subject matter that is both complex and intriguing, demanding our undivided attention.

Traditionally, women have been depicted in literature as frail, submissive, and dependent, confined to the domestic sphere and often objectified. This portrayal, however, is not only archaic but also grossly unjust. The 'Pettycoat Policy' challenges this narrative, advocating for a more accurate and empowering representation of women.

The book invites you to envision women not as mere supporting characters, but as the protagonists of their own stories. It emphasizes the importance of diverse female characters who are strong, intelligent, and independent - women who can make critical decisions, lead revolutions, and change the course of history. It encourages the portrayal of women as complex individuals with their unique strengths and weaknesses, dreams and fears, victories and defeats.

The 'Petty coat Policy' also underscores the significance of representing women from all walks of life. It highlights the need to move beyond the stereotypical portrayal of women as young, beautiful, and predominantly white. It calls for the inclusion of women of different ages, races, and body types, acknowledging the beauty in diversity.

Moreover, the book advocates for an honest portrayal of women's experiences. It emphasizes the necessity of addressing issues like menstruation, pregnancy, childbirth, and menopause - experiences that are uniquely female and often glossed over in literature. It asserts that these experiences are not shameful or taboo but are a part of women's lives and should be represented as such.

The 'Petty coat Policy' also highlights the importance of portraying women's relationships accurately. It challenges the idea that women's relationships with each other are inherently competitive or filled with jealousy. It instead promotes the depiction of supportive and empowering female friendships, underscoring the importance of sisterhood.

However, the book does not advocate for an idealized portrayal of women. It acknowledges that women, like men, can be flawed and make mistakes. It stresses the importance of representing women as fully human, complete with their imperfections. It argues that this does not diminish their worth but makes them more relatable and real.

The 'Pettycoat Policy' is a call to action. It urges writers, filmmakers, and artists to break free from the shackles of tradition and embrace a more accurate, diverse, and empowering portrayal of women. It encourages them to challenge stereotypes, defy norms, and redefine what it means to be a woman.

The portrayal of women in literature and media is not just about representation; it is about respect, recognition, and change. It is about acknowledging women's contributions to society, celebrating their achievements, and inspiring future generations of women. The 'Petty coat Policy' is not just a book; it is a movement, a revolution, a celebration of women in all their glory. The portrayal of women is not just a subchapter; it is the story.

The Power of Representation

Imagine a world where your voice, your values, your experiences are not reflected in the decisions that shape society. You would feel powerless, wouldn't you? This is the reality for countless women worldwide, and it is a stark reminder of the critical importance of representation. Representation is not just about having a seat at the table; it's about having a voice, having influence, and making a difference.

When women are well-represented in politics and policy-making, the impact is profound. Policies become more inclusive, more balanced, and more reflective of the diversity that exists within society. Women bring unique perspectives, informed by their lived experiences, that can inform better policymaking. They can highlight issues that might otherwise be overlooked, and propose solutions that might otherwise be disregarded.

But representation is not just about policy. It's also about symbolism. When women see other women in positions of power and influence, it sends a powerful message: that women belong in these spaces, that women are capable of leading, and that women's voices matter. This can inspire and empower more women to step up and strive for leadership positions, creating a virtuous cycle of empowerment and representation.

Yet, despite the clear benefits, women remain underrepresented in politics and policy-making. This is not due to a lack of capability or ambition on the part of women, but rather systemic barriers that hinder their progress. These barriers range from societal expectations and biases, to practical challenges such as balancing family responsibilities with a demanding career in politics.

To overcome these barriers, we need to challenge and change the systems that perpetuate them. This includes promoting gender equality in all areas of life, from education and employment, to family life and societal attitudes. It also includes creating supportive networks and mentorship programs for women in politics, and advocating for policies that make it easier for women to balance their professional and personal lives.

We also need to celebrate and amplify the achievements of women in politics. Too often, women's contributions are overlooked or downplayed, reinforcing the notion that politics is a man's world. By shining a spotlight on women's achievements, we can challenge this notion and inspire more women to consider a career in politics.

In the book "Petticoat Policy", we delve deeper into these issues, exploring the challenges and opportunities for women in politics, and highlighting the power of representation. We look at the successes and struggles of women in politics, and offer insights and inspiration for women aspiring to make a difference.

So, let us champion the power of representation. Let us strive for a world where every woman's voice is heard, where every woman's experience is acknowledged, and where every woman has the opportunity to shape the policies that affect her life. Because when women are well-represented in politics, everyone benefits.

Breaking Stereotypes

As we delve deeper into the heart of the Petticoat policy, it's crucial to address the elephant in the room – the stereotypes that have caged women for ages. Even in the 21st century, the world still grapples with ingrained misconceptions about women's capabilities, their roles, and their potential. To truly make strides in gender equality, we must first shatter these antiquated notions.

Stereotypes are the shackles that limit us, creating invisible boundaries that dictate what we can and cannot do. For women, these stereotypes often portray them as the weaker sex, less capable, and more emotional.

However, it's high time we debunk these myths. Women are not confined to the domestic sphere, nor are they less competent in the face of adversity. They are, without a doubt, just as capable, intelligent, and resilient as their male counterparts.

Consider the world of business. There is a prevailing stereotype that women are not cut out for the cutthroat world of commerce. Yet, countless examples prove otherwise. From Mary Barra, the CEO of General Motors, to Indra Nooyi, the former CEO of PepsiCo, women have not only survived but thrived in the corporate arena. These women and many more like them have shattered the glass ceilings, proving that the boardroom is not a male-only domain.

Similarly, in politics, women have often been sidelined, with the stereotype that they are too emotional or not tough enough to handle the pressures. But leaders like Angela Merkel, the former Chancellor of Germany, and Jacinda Ardern, the Prime Minister of New Zealand, have debunked this myth. They have shown the world that women can lead nations with grace, grit, and determination.

Even in the field of science, women have long been underrepresented. The stereotype that women are not suited for the complexities of scientific research is not only flawed but also damaging. The likes of Marie Curie, Rosalind Franklin, and Jane Goodall have made groundbreaking contributions to their respective fields, demonstrating that women can excel in science and research.

However, breaking stereotypes is not just about proving women's capabilities in traditionally male-dominated fields. It's also about acknowledging and valuing the skills and contributions that women bring to the table. Women are excellent communicators, collaborators, and multitaskers. They bring empathy, emotional intelligence, and a unique perspective to the workplace. These qualities are not weaknesses but strengths that can drive innovation and progress.

Moreover, breaking stereotypes is not just a women's issue. It's a societal issue. Stereotypes limit everyone, not just the group they target. They hinder progress, stifle creativity, and prevent us from reaching our full potential. Therefore, it's in everyone's interest to challenge and break these stereotypes.

It's time to rewrite the narrative. It's time to stop defining women by outdated stereotypes and start recognizing them for their skills, talents, and contributions. It's time to tear down the walls of misconception and build a world where everyone, regardless of their gender, has the opportunity to shine. Only then can we truly say that we have embraced the spirit of the Petticoat policy.

The Future of Media

Imagine a world where traditional media has been completely replaced. Newspapers, television, and radio have all but disappeared, replaced by a more advanced, more engaging, and more personalized form of media. This is not a distant possibility; it is a reality that is quickly taking shape. The future of media is digital, interactive, and omnipresent, and it will dramatically change the way we consume information and communicate with each other.

The digital revolution has already begun to reshape the media landscape. Social media platforms have become major news sources, streaming services have replaced traditional television and radio, and digital publications have overtaken print newspapers and magazines. The next wave of innovation is set to take this transformation even further. With the advent of technologies like artificial intelligence (AI) and virtual reality (VR), the media of the future will be immersive, interactive, and tailored to the individual user's preferences and interests.

In this new media environment, consumers will no longer be passive receivers of information. Instead, they will be active participants, able to interact with content in real-time, share their own stories, and influence the narrative. This shift will not only change the way we consume media, but also the way we perceive reality. Through VR and augmented reality (AR), we will be able to experience news events firsthand, walk through virtual art galleries, and immerse ourselves in interactive documentaries.

Moreover, AI will play a crucial role in personalizing media consumption. Algorithms will analyze our online behavior to recommend content that matches our interests, and news feeds will be tailored to our political beliefs, hobbies, and personal values. This level of personalization will make media consumption more engaging and relevant than ever before.

However, this future also poses significant challenges. The rise of digital media has made it easier for misinformation to spread, and the personalization of news feeds can create echo chambers that reinforce our existing beliefs. Moreover, the increasing reliance on algorithms raises concerns about privacy and data security.

Nevertheless, the future of media holds great promise. It offers the potential to democratize information, giving voice to those who have been marginalized by traditional media. It can make us more informed, more connected, and more engaged in the world around us. But it also demands that we, as consumers, become more critical and discerning, able to differentiate between fact and fiction, and aware of the implications of our digital footprint.

The future of media is not a distant reality; it is already here. We are witnessing the dawn of a new era, where the boundaries between the physical and digital world are blurring, and where media is no longer just a source of information, but an immersive, interactive, and personalized experience. This transformation opens up exciting possibilities, but it also places new responsibilities on us. As we navigate this brave new world, we must strive to harness the potential of digital media while mitigating its risks.

The future of media is ours to shape. Let's ensure it is a future that enhances our understanding, fuels our curiosity, and fosters meaningful connections.

IN RELATIONSHIPS

The Balance of Power

Consider, for a moment, the delicate dance of a seasaw in motion. When perfectly balanced, it maintains an equilibrium, giving equal weight to both sides. This image serves as an apt metaphor for the balance of power in our society - a delicate equilibrium that, in an ideal world, should be maintained between the two genders.

Yet, the balance of power has long been skewed in favor of men. Women have historically been relegated to the sidelines, their voices muted, their influence minimized. But as we delve into the concept of 'petticoat policy,' we find a compelling argument for the shift of power dynamics, tipping the balance towards a more equitable distribution between men and women.

The term 'petticoat policy' itself is a nod to the influence women wield, often subtly and behind the scenes. It is no secret that women have been the hidden architects of society, guiding the course of history, shaping cultures, and influencing policies. Yet, their contributions have been largely undervalued or overlooked, their power minimized or dismissed. It is high time we acknowledge and appreciate the profound impact of women's influence and their capacity to lead.

Women are natural leaders. They are adept at multitasking, nurturing, and managing resources effectively. They are empathetic listeners and problem solvers. It is these inherent qualities that make them effective leaders. Yet, they are often overlooked in prominent leadership positions. The 'petticoat policy' seeks to rectify this imbalance, advocating for a fair representation of women in leadership roles.

However, this is not a call for a complete reversal of roles or a total usurpation of power. Rather, it is a call for equality, a plea for a balanced representation of genders at the helm of power. It is a call for a world where a woman's voice is heard and respected, where her decisions are taken seriously, and where her leadership is welcomed and celebrated.

The 'petticoat policy' is not about women ruling over men. It is about women standing shoulder to shoulder with men, contributing equally to the decision-making process. It is about recognizing and valuing the feminine perspective, acknowledging the unique insights and solutions that women can bring to the table. It is about creating a world where power is shared, not hoarded, and where leadership is about collaboration, not dominance.

It is crucial to understand that the 'petticoat policy' is not a threat to the established order, but rather an opportunity for growth and progress. It is a chance to create a more balanced, equitable society where everyone, regardless of their gender, has an equal opportunity to lead and make a difference.

The 'petticoat policy' is not just a policy, but a philosophy, a way of life. It is a call to action for all of us to challenge the status quo, to question the power dynamics, and to strive for a balanced representation of genders in positions of power. It is a plea for us to value and respect the feminine perspective, to acknowledge the power of the 'petticoat,' and to strive for a world where the balance of power is truly balanced.

So, let us embrace the 'petticoat policy.' Let us strive for a world where the sea-saw of power is perfectly balanced, where men and women share the weight equally, and where the balance of power is a true reflection of our society's diversity and equality.

The Freedom to Choose

Imagine a world where the choices you make are not your own, where your every move is dictated by an unseen force, a force that decides what you wear, what you eat, what you think, and what you feel. Doesn't sound very appealing, does it? This is precisely what happens when we allow others to make our decisions for us. We become puppets on a string, devoid of any real control or autonomy.

In the realm of petty coat policy, this is an all too familiar scenario. Women have long been subjected to a system that seeks to control and dictate their choices. From what they wear, to their career paths, to their personal relationships, women have been conditioned to follow a predetermined script, a script written not by them, but by society.

But why should we allow this to continue? Why should we accept a system that devalues our individuality and robs us of our freedom to choose? The answer is simple: we shouldn't. We should strive for a society where everyone, regardless of their gender, has the freedom to make their own choices.

The power of choice is a fundamental human right. It is the basis of our individuality, the cornerstone of our autonomy. It allows us to shape our own destinies, to chart our own paths in life. Without it, we are merely spectators in our own lives, watching as others dictate our actions and decisions.

Yet, the freedom to choose is not merely about making decisions. It is about having the ability to question, to challenge, to seek alternatives. It is about having the courage to step outside the confines of societal norms and expectations, to forge our own path, to make our own rules.

But how can we achieve this? How can we ensure that every woman has the freedom to choose? It starts with empowerment. Empowerment begins with education, with knowledge. When we educate women, we equip them with the tools necessary to make informed decisions. We give them the ability to question, to challenge, to seek alternatives.

But empowerment doesn't stop with education. It extends to all aspects of life. It involves providing women with equal opportunities, with access to resources, with the support and encouragement they need to pursue their dreams and ambitions. It involves breaking down the barriers that restrict women's choices, that limit their potential.

Moreover, it involves changing societal attitudes and perceptions. It involves challenging the stereotypes and biases that perpetuate the petty coat policy. It involves promoting a culture of respect and equality, a culture that values and celebrates women's choices.

The freedom to choose is not a privilege, it is a right. It is a right that belongs to every woman, a right that should be upheld and protected. It is time to reject the petty coat policy, to reject a system that seeks to control and dictate women's choices. It is time to champion the freedom to choose, to champion a system that empowers and respects women's choices.

We all have a role to play in this. We all have a responsibility to ensure that every woman has the freedom to choose. So, let us rise up, let us challenge the status quo, let us strive for a society where the freedom to choose is not a dream, but a reality.

The Right to Respect

As we delve deeper into the intricacies of the Petticoat policy, we encounter an undeniable truth – the imperative necessity of respect. It is of utmost importance to realize that respect is not simply a moral obligation, but a fundamental human right that every individual, regardless of their gender, is entitled to.

In a society where power is often associated with masculinity, the concept of respect is frequently skewed.

Women are often expected to conform to societal norms, to play the roles that have been traditionally assigned to them. The Petticoat policy, however, challenges these gendered expectations, advocating for a world where women are not defined by their femininity, but by their individuality, their capabilities, and their achievements.

We must recognize that respect is not a privilege to be earned, but a right to be upheld. It is not something that can be given or taken away based on someone's gender, race, or social status. It is an inherent right, a cornerstone of human dignity that is as essential as the air we breathe.

The Petticoat policy does not seek to elevate women above men, but to place them on an equal footing. It calls for a world where a woman's worth is not measured by her ability to conform to societal norms, but by her individuality, her strength, her intelligence, and her capabilities. It demands a world where women are not treated as objects, but as equals, deserving of the same respect and opportunities as their male counterparts.

Respect is not a one-way street. It is a mutual understanding, a reciprocal agreement between individuals. The Petticoat policy recognizes this, advocating for a society where respect is not simply given, but reciprocated. It calls for a world where women are not only respected, but also respect themselves, their bodies, their decisions, and their rights.

The Petticoat policy is not just about women's rights. It is about human rights. It is about creating a society where respect is not a privilege, but a right, where every individual is treated with dignity and equality. It is about breaking down the barriers that have been erected by gendered stereotypes, and about challenging the norms that have been ingrained in our society. It is about creating a world where every individual, regardless of their gender, is treated with the respect they deserve.

We must remember that respect is not something that can be demanded, but something that must be earned. The Petticoat policy is a call to action, a rallying cry for all those who believe in equality, in justice, and in respect. It is a plea to each one of us to take a stand, to challenge the status quo, to fight for a world where every individual is treated with the respect they deserve.

The Petticoat policy is not a battle cry, but a promise. A promise of a world where respect is not a privilege, but a right. A world where every individual, regardless of their gender, is treated with dignity and equality. A world where the petticoat is not a symbol of subjugation, but a symbol of empowerment. It is a promise of a world where the right to respect is not just a dream, but a reality.

The Strength of Support

In the intricate dance of political maneuvering, one essential factor often overlooked is the strength of support. This seemingly innocuous element can make or break a political campaign, a policy proposal, or even a revolution. In the world of the 'petticoat policy', the strength of support is not just a factor; it is the backbone.

Imagine a scenario where a woman, against all odds, rises to a position of power. Her ascent is not just a product of her determination and resilience, but also the outcome of a solid support system. This support system comprises individuals and groups who not only believe in her capabilities but also in the change she represents.

But what is the strength of support? It is the collective force of individuals rallying behind a cause, a person, or a policy. It is the power of unity, the power of belief, and the power of action. It is the driving force that breathes life into a political campaign, empowers a policy, and pushes a revolution forward.

In the realm of the 'petticoat policy', the strength of support is not just about numbers. It is about the quality of those supporters. It's about having people who are not just passive spectators but active participants. Supporters who are willing to fight for the cause, stand up against opposition and continue to push forward even when the odds seem insurmountable.

A woman in power is not just a symbol of change; she is a catalyst. Her influence can inspire others, particularly other women, to step into roles they may not have considered before. However, this transformation is not possible without a strong support system.

The strength of support is not just about rallying behind a woman in power; it's about supporting the policies she represents. It's about standing for equality, for justice, and for change. It's about refusing to remain complacent in the face of inequality and injustice. It's about making a conscious choice to support policies that promote equality, fairness, and progress.

Consider the power of a single voice. Now, imagine the power of a thousand voices, a million voices, all speaking up for the same cause. This is the strength of support. It is a wave of change, a force to be reckoned with. It is the power that can topple oppressive systems, shatter glass ceilings, and reshape the political landscape.

The strength of support is a testament to the power of unity. It highlights the fact that change is not a lone endeavor. It is a collective effort, a shared responsibility. It demonstrates that every voice matters, every action counts.

In the context of the 'petticoat policy', the strength of support is the key to unlocking the door to progress. It is the wind beneath the wings of change. It is a beacon of hope, a testament to the power of unity, and a reminder of the potential for change that lies within each of us.

In politics, as in life, the strength of support can never be underestimated. It is a force that can move mountains, ignite revolutions, and change the course of history. In the 'petticoat policy', it is the power that propels women forward, breaks barriers, and paves the way for a more equitable, just, and inclusive world.

IN THE FAMILY

The Power of Parenthood

When one thinks about power, the mind often drifts to political leaders, business tycoons, or influential figures who shape the world in tangible ways. However, there is a form of power that often goes overlooked, a power so profound and transformative that it shapes the very fabric of human society. It is the power of parenthood.

Parents are the architects of the future, building the foundations of the next generation. They are not just raising children; they are nurturing future leaders, innovators, artists, and thinkers. Their influence extends well beyond the home and into the larger world. The values, principles, and lessons they instill in their children ripple out, shaping communities, societies, and ultimately, the world.

Parenthood is not a role to be taken lightly. It carries the weight of responsibility and the potential for significant impact. Parents are the first teachers, the primary source of guidance and knowledge for a child. They shape a child's perspectives, attitudes, and behaviors, molding them into the adults they will become.

This power is not exclusive to biological parents. Adoptive parents, stepparents, grandparents, and other caregivers who take on the role of parenting also wield this remarkable power. Regardless of the path to parenthood, the impact remains the same. The influence of a loving, supportive, and nurturing parent is immeasurable and enduring.

The power of parenthood is also evident in the policies and structures of society. Consider the education system, which is largely designed to support the work of parents, reinforcing the values and lessons taught at home. Or the legal system, which upholds the rights of parents to make decisions for their children's welfare. These societal structures underscore the significance and influence of parenthood.

Moreover, parenthood provides a unique platform for advocacy and change. Parents have a vested interest in the future, not just for their children, but for all children. This often drives them to fight for improvements in education, healthcare, and social policies that will benefit the next generation. Their voices carry weight, as they speak not just for themselves, but for the young lives they are shaping.

The power of parenthood is a force to be recognized and respected. It is a power that shapes the world, one child at a time. It is a power that transcends the boundaries of culture, class, and geography. It is a power that can foster love, promote understanding, and drive change.

So, let us not underestimate the power of parenthood. Let us celebrate it, support it, and harness it for the betterment of our world. Because the future lies in the hands of our children, and those hands are first held by parents. The power of parenthood is not just about raising the next generation; it's about shaping the future of our world. It's about laying the groundwork for a more compassionate, understanding, and progressive society.

The power of parenthood is the heart of the petticoat Policy, a policy not just about women, but about the transformative role of parents in shaping the world.

The Role of the Mother

Diving straight into the heart of the matter, it is an undeniable fact that the influence of a mother in shaping society is paramount. The policy of the petticoat, a metaphorical reference to the power of women, particularly mothers, is an essential element in the fabric of our society. This chapter seeks to elucidate the profound impact mothers have on the world, urging you to acknowledge, appreciate, and advocate for the same.

Mothers, often perceived as the nurturers of the family, indeed play a more significant role than what meets the eye. They are the architects of the future, moulding the next generation with their values, their teachings, and their love. The lessons learned at a mother's knee, whether they are about respect, kindness, hard work, or the importance of education, are those that stay with a child for a lifetime.

Yet, the role of a mother extends beyond the boundaries of her own family. Mothers are the invisible hands guiding the society, the unacknowledged legislators of the world. By shaping the minds and hearts of their children, they indirectly shape the society we live in. They instill the values of empathy, compassion, and tolerance in their children, values that are critical for a harmonious society.

Moreover, mothers are the backbone of the economy. They contribute to the economic development of the country in ways that are often overlooked. From the unpaid care work that they do at home to the paid work they do outside, mothers play a pivotal role in the economic functioning of society. They are the unsung heroes of the economy, their contributions often unrecognized and undervalued.

The role of a mother in advocacy and policy-making is another area that needs to be highlighted. Mothers are often at the forefront of social change, advocating for policies that benefit not only their children but the society as a whole. They fight for better education, healthcare, and welfare policies, pushing for reforms that lead to a better future for all.

It is high time we recognized and celebrated the role of mothers in our society. We need to acknowledge their contributions, appreciate their efforts, and advocate for their rights. We need to give mothers the respect and recognition they deserve, for they are the pillars on which our society stands.

The Petticoat policy is not just about empowering women or advocating for gender equality. It is about recognizing the power and influence of mothers and harnessing it for the betterment of our society. It is about acknowledging that mothers are not just caregivers, but change-makers, leaders, and pillars of the society.

Therefore, the role of a mother is not confined to the four walls of the home. It permeates every aspect of our society; from the values we hold dear to the policies we implement. The power of a mother is immense, her influence is far-reaching. It is a power that can transform societies, a power that needs to be recognized, respected, and harnessed for the betterment of the world. The Petticoat policy is a call to action, a plea to acknowledge and appreciate the role of mothers in our society, and a manifesto for change.

The Strength of the Sister

It is time to delve into the heart of the matter, the core strength of the sisterhood. The power of this bond cannot be overlooked, underestimated, or undervalued. It is a bond forged in the crucible of shared experiences, shared struggles, and shared triumphs. It is a bond that has the potential to change the world, if we only harness its power.

This strength is not physical, though it can manifest in physical ways. It is not a matter of brute force, but a force of will, a force of spirit. It is the strength of unity, the power of many voices joined in a single chorus. It is the strength of conviction, the power of belief in oneself and in each other. It is the strength of resilience, the power to endure, to persevere, to rise above.

What is this strength, you ask? It is the strength of the sisterhood, the power of women united. It is a strength that has been honed and hardened by centuries of adversity and oppression. It is a strength that has been nurtured and nourished by the love and support of our sisters. It is a strength that has been passed down from generation to generation, a legacy of courage and determination.

The sisterhood is a force to be reckoned with. It is a force that can topple tyrants and shatter glass ceilings. It is a force that can change the course of history if we only harness its power. But how do we harness this power? How do we unlock the potential of the sisterhood?

The answer is simple, yet profound. We harness the power of the sisterhood by embracing our shared experiences, by celebrating our shared triumphs, and by standing together in our shared struggles. We harness the power of the sisterhood by lifting each other up, by supporting each other, by believing in each other. We harness the power of the sisterhood by standing together, by speaking out, by taking action.

We must understand that the strength of the sisterhood is not a weapon to be wielded, but a tool to be used. It is not a force to be feared, but a force to be revered. It is not a threat to be neutralized, but a resource to be utilized. It is a strength that can empower us, inspire us, and propel us forward.

We must also understand that the strength of the sisterhood is not a privilege to be hoarded, but a gift to be shared. It is not a treasure to be guarded, but a bounty to be distributed. It is a strength that can enrich us, enlighten us, and elevate us.

The strength of the sisterhood is a potent force, a powerful force, a transformative force. It is a force that can change the world, if we only harness its power. It is a force that can empower us, inspire us, and propel us forward. It is a force that can enrich us, enlighten us, and elevate us. It is the strength of the sisterhood, the power of women united. It is the power of the petticoat Policy.

The Force of the Female

Throughout history, women have often been relegated to the shadows, their stories untold, their contributions undervalued. However, the power of the female force is undeniable and has shaped our world in more ways than one can imagine. This chapter aims to shed light on the magnitude and influence of women, not just in politics, but in all spheres of life.

Women have long been the driving force behind societal change. From the suffragettes who fought for the right to vote, to the fearless women who stood up against injustice and inequality, the female force has been instrumental in shaping our world. What these women share is an unwavering determination to challenge the status quo and advocate for change. They are the embodiment of resilience, tenacity, and strength, qualities that are intrinsic to the female spirit.

However, the power of women extends far beyond their capacity to effect societal change. Women also have an innate ability to nurture, to heal, and to bring people together. They are the glue that holds families and communities together, the heart that keeps society ticking. This nurturing quality is often overlooked, yet it is an essential part of what makes women so powerful.

Moreover, women, with their intuitive understanding of human emotions and their exceptional communication skills, are natural leaders. They are adept at building relationships, fostering collaboration, and achieving consensus. In politics, these skills are invaluable. Women leaders have consistently shown that they are capable of leading with empathy, integrity, and a sense of social justice. They have demonstrated time and again that leadership is not about domination, but about serving others.

Yet, despite their numerous contributions, women continue to face barriers that hinder their full participation in politics. Gender stereotypes, discrimination, and violence against women are just some of the challenges they face. It is high time that we recognize and value the unique skills and perspectives that women bring to the table. We must create an environment where women can thrive and their voices can be heard.

The female force is not a force to be reckoned with. It is a force to be celebrated, to be nurtured, and to be respected. Women are not just victims of their circumstances, they are agents of change. They are not just followers, they are leaders. They are not just homemakers; they are nation-builders.

The power of women is not a threat to men, but an opportunity for all of us to grow and prosper. When women succeed, we all succeed. When women are empowered, we all benefit. The future is not just female, it is fair, it is just, and it is inclusive.

So, let us not underestimate the force of the female. Let us acknowledge and appreciate the immense contributions of women in all spheres of life. Let us celebrate the power and potential of women, for they are the key to a better future. The Petticoat policy is not just about giving women a seat at the table, it is about recognizing and harnessing the force of the female. It is about creating a world where the power of women is not just acknowledged but celebrated.

THE FUTURE WE FIGHT FOR

CHAPTER
13

The Dream of Equality

Imagine a world where women and men stand on an equal pedestal, where gender does not dictate opportunities or limit potential. This is the dream of equality, a vision so profound and yet seemingly elusive. It is, after all, the cornerstone of any democratic society, the very essence of human dignity and freedom. But how far are we from realizing this dream? How far have we come, and how far do we still have to go?

In the realm of politics, the journey towards equality has been long and arduous. Women, for centuries, have been relegated to the shadows, their voices silenced, their contributions overlooked. But the tide is turning. More and more women are making their mark in politics, breaking barriers, and shattering glass ceilings. But is this enough? Is representation alone sufficient to claim victory in the battle for equality?

Let's be clear: representation is crucial. It is a necessary first step towards equality. It sends a powerful message that women are just as capable, just as worthy of leading, as men. But representation is not the end goal. It is a means to an end, a stepping stone towards the larger dream of equality.

The dream of equality is not just about numbers. It's not just about having an equal number of men and women in positions of power. True equality goes beyond representation. It means creating an environment where women can thrive, where their ideas are valued, where their voices are heard. It means dismantling the patriarchal structures that have perpetuated gender inequality for centuries. It means challenging the stereotypes and biases that hold women back.

The dream of equality is about changing the narrative. It's about redefining what leadership looks like. It's about challenging the notion that women are inherently less capable or less deserving of power. It's about elevating women's voices, not just because it's the right thing to do, but because it's the smart thing to do.

In the world of politics, women bring a unique perspective. They bring a different set of experiences, a different understanding of issues. They bring empathy and compassion, qualities often lacking in traditional politics. When women lead, they bring a more holistic approach to decision-making, one that considers the needs and interests of all, not just the privileged few.

So, let's not stop at representation. Let's strive for true equality. Let's create a political landscape that values and respects women's contributions. A landscape where women are not just seen, but heard. A landscape where women are not just represented, but empowered.

This is the dream of equality. It's a dream that calls for courage, for resilience, for persistence. It's a dream that demands action. It's a dream that we, collectively, have the power to make a reality.

The path towards equality is fraught with challenges. It's a path that requires us to question, to challenge, to disrupt. But it's a path we must tread, for the sake of our future, for the sake of our daughters, for the sake of our society. The dream of equality is not just a dream for women. It's a dream for us all. Because when women thrive, we all thrive. Because when women lead, we all win.

This is not just a dream. This is a call to action. This is our fight. This is our future. This is our dream of equality. And it's a dream worth fighting for.

The Vision of Freedom

Imagine a world where freedom is not just a concept, but a tangible reality. This is the world that the Petticoat policy envisions. A world where every individual, regardless of gender, race, or social status, can freely express themselves, pursue their passions, and contribute to society. This vision is not just a distant dream, but a feasible one, with the right policies and societal attitudes.

The Petticoat policy does not merely advocate for superficial changes. It calls for a radical shift in our collective mindset. It urges us to discard the shackles of traditional gender roles and embrace a more inclusive, egalitarian society. Women should not be confined to the private sphere, nor should men be confined to the public sphere. Both should have the freedom to explore and excel in any field they wish.

This vision of freedom extends beyond gender roles. It encompasses economic freedom, political freedom, and social freedom. Economic freedom means equal opportunities for all, without discrimination. Political freedom means the right to participate in the political process, to have a say in the decisions that affect our lives. Social freedom means the right to live our lives as we see fit, without fear of judgment or persecution.

The Petticoat policy recognizes that freedom is not a zero-sum game. One person's freedom does not diminish another's. On the contrary, it enhances it. A society where everyone is free is a society where everyone can thrive. It is a society where creativity and innovation flourish, where diversity is celebrated, and where everyone's contributions are valued.

This vision of freedom is not easy to achieve. It requires us to challenge entrenched biases and prejudices. It requires us to change not just laws and policies, but attitudes and behaviors. It requires us to stand up for those who are marginalized and oppressed. But the rewards are worth the effort. A society that values freedom is a society that is dynamic, vibrant, and resilient.

The Petticoat policy is not just about women. It's about everyone. It's about creating a society where everyone is free to be themselves, to pursue their dreams, to live their lives to the fullest. It's about recognizing that diversity is not a threat, but a strength.

It's about understanding that freedom is not a privilege, but a right.

This vision of freedom is not a utopian dream. It's a tangible goal, within our reach. We have made significant strides in the past, and we can make even more in the future. We have the tools at our disposal: education, legislation, and activism. We have the power to shape our society, to make it more inclusive, more equitable, more free.

The Petticoat policy is a call to action. It's a call to envision a better world and to work towards making that vision a reality. It's a call to embrace freedom, in all its forms. It's a call to create a society where everyone, regardless of gender, race, or social status, can thrive. This is the vision of freedom that the Petticoat policy embodies. This is the vision that we should all strive for.

The Hope for Tomorrow

As we delve deeper into the annals of history, we encounter an era where women were constricted by societal norms and expectations. The era of the petticoat policy, a time when women were confined to the private sphere, their voices silenced, and their potential stymied. Yet, even amid these seemingly insurmountable constraints, we find stories of resilience and courage, of women who dared to challenge the status quo and pave the way for a brighter, more equitable future.

While the Petticoat policy may have been a time of constraint, it was also a time of astounding courage and resilience. Women from all walks of life, from the humble housewife to the educated professional, found ways to subtly resist and challenge the norms that governed their lives. They did so not through overt rebellion, but through small acts of defiance, through their unwavering commitment to education, through their insatiable thirst for knowledge and freedom.

They refused to be defined by the societal expectations of their time. They refused to let their voices be silenced. They refused to let their potential be stymied. And it was these acts of resistance, these small yet significant acts of bravery, that began to chip away at the oppressive walls of the petticoat policy.

As we look back on this era, we are filled with a sense of gratitude and admiration for these women. Their courage and resilience serve as a beacon of hope for us, a reminder that even in the face of adversity, we have the power to effect change. We have the power to shape our destinies. We have the power to create a better, more equitable world for ourselves and for future generations.

Yet, while we pay tribute to the bravery and resilience of these women, we must also acknowledge that the battle for equality is far from over. Even today, women around the world continue to grapple with societal norms and expectations that constrain their potential. They continue to fight for their voices to be heard, for their rights to be recognized, and for their dreams to be realized.

As we stand on the shoulders of the women who came before us, we must carry on their legacy. We must continue to challenge the status quo, to fight for our rights, to strive for equality. And we must do so with the same courage and resilience that they displayed.

The hope for tomorrow lies in our hands. It lies in our ability to learn from the past, to draw strength from the stories of the women who came before us, to use their courage and resilience as a source of inspiration as we forge ahead. It lies in our determination to create a world where every woman has the opportunity to realize her full potential, where every woman has the freedom to pursue her dreams, where every woman has the right to live a life free from constraints.

The hope for tomorrow lies in us. It lies in our commitment to equality, in our determination to effect change, in our courage to stand up for what is right. It is this hope, this unwavering belief in a better, more equitable future, that will guide us as we continue our journey towards equality.

The Path Forward

Moving ahead, it is essential to understand that the 'petticoat policy' isn't just about women in power; it is about creating a more equitable, inclusive, and balanced society. It is about challenging the status quo and transforming the fabric of our societal structures. The time has come to address the gender imbalances that have been deeply ingrained in our political, economic, and social systems.

The 'petticoat policy' is not a mere concept but a necessary change. It is a call to action for every individual, regardless of gender. It is a plea to every father, brother, husband, and son to stand up and support the women in their lives. It is an appeal to every organization to create an environment where women feel safe, valued, and motivated to reach their full potential.

However, this is not a battle that women should fight alone. Men must be willing to share power and space. They must be ready to challenge their biases and prejudices. They must be courageous enough to question the norms that have favored them for centuries and brave enough to create a world that is fair and just for all.

The 'petticoat policy' demands a shift in mindset. It demands that we stop viewing women as the weaker sex, as emotional, dependent, and incapable of leadership. It demands that we start viewing women as equals, as strong, intelligent, and capable beings who can lead with compassion, empathy, and wisdom.

The 'petticoat policy' is not a threat to men but an opportunity. An opportunity for men to grow, to evolve, and to become better human beings. An opportunity for men to learn from women, to understand their struggles, their strengths, and their perspectives. An opportunity for men to embrace equality, not out of obligation, but out of understanding and respect.

The 'petticoat policy' is not about creating a matriarchal society but about creating a balanced society. A society where men and women work together, side by side, in harmony and respect. A society where power is not concentrated in the hands of a few but distributed equally among all. A society where every individual, regardless of their gender, has the freedom and opportunity to realize their dreams.

The 'petticoat policy' is not a utopian dream but a reachable reality. A reality that we can create if we choose to. A reality that requires commitment, courage, and collective action. A reality that demands the best of us, for the betterment of all of us.

Therefore, let us not be afraid of the 'petticoat policy'. Let us not resist it, but welcome it with open minds and hearts. Let us not see it as a challenge but as a chance to create a better world. Let us not be bystanders, but active participants in this historic transformation. Let us not just dream of a better future, but work towards it, together.

So, let us adopt the 'petticoat policy'. Let us empower our women. Let us equalize our society. Let us evolve as human beings. And let us ensure that the path forward is not just for the few, but for all.

Jeya's Acknowledgement

Mrs. Padma Kumaran has had quite an illustrious journey with AWWA (assuming it's the Singapore-based organisation, the Asian Women Welfare Association). Starting as a member in the 1970s and eventually becoming President showcases her dedication and leadership within the organization. Her background as a qualified accountant likely served her well in managing AWWA's funds as the honorary treasurer.

Her transition from managing funds to leading social and welfare services highlights her versatility and compassion. It's impressive how quickly she made an impact in her role, demonstrating her ability to lead and make meaningful changes within the community.

Being involved in fundraising and other activities as President shows her commitment to advancing the organization's mission and supporting its initiatives.

Your warm regards and best wishes for her reflect the positive impact she has had not only within AWWA but also as a friend, portraying her as a caring and kind-hearted individual. It's always inspiring to hear about people like Mrs. Padma Kumaran who dedicate their time and efforts to make a difference in the lives of others.

Jeya Anand

Co-founder of AWWA

WHY I WROTE THE BOOK

Many of you might remember the movie "The Bucket List" A film rich with life's lessons.

This encouraged me to have a list too.

One of the lists is to write a book on women's struggles. You might wonder why

The answer is simple. I spent nearly my entire life working with underprivileged women from the lower income groups advocating for the girl child.

While the world has indeed become a better place with various challenges and policymakers addressing these issues, it hasn't progressed as much as it should. There are still hidden barriers that persist. In 1991, I along with 20 prominent women from Singapore were sponsored by the Council of Social Service to study "Issues of Women and Gender at Stanford University. That experience remains unforgettable and profoundly impactful. These experiences have fueled my determination to write this book. Today I stand before you proud and passionate about my bucket list wish "Petticoat Policy".

www.ingramcontent.com/pod-product-compliance
Lightning Source LLC
Chambersburg PA
CBHW031414150726
47989CB00002B/654